THE ATONEMENT
IN THE LIGHT OF HISTORY
AND THE MODERN SPIRIT

THE ATONEMENT
IN THE LIGHT OF HISTORY AND
THE MODERN SPIRIT

BY THE REV.

DAVID SMITH, D.D.

PROFESSOR OF THEOLOGY IN THE

M'CREA MAGEE COLLEGE, LONDONDERRY

'And He said unto them, Therefore every
scribe who hath been made a disciple to the
Kingdom of Heaven is like unto a man that is
a householder, which bringeth forth out of his
treasure things new and old.'—ST. MATT. xiii. 52.

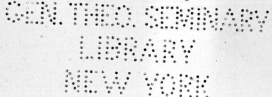
HODDER AND STOUGHTON
LONDON   NEW YORK   TORONTO

PREFACE

FOR years it has been my privilege to receive inquiries from perplexed souls near and far on problems of faith and conduct, and to answer these, according to my ability, in the *British Weekly*; and there is none which has been more frequently presented to me than the question of the Atonement, especially during those dark years of our nation's and the world's anguish. The sorrow of the War has discovered our sore need of the Saviour; and laymen have written to me complaining that they never now hear the Gospel of the Redeeming Sacrifice, while ministers have told me that they would fain preach it but it is a puzzle to them. It is felt that the doctrines hitherto received are no longer possible;

> ' And what can helpers heal
> With old-world cures men half believe
> For woes they wholly feel ? '

And the books which are written nowadays
are either negative criticisms *ad nauseam* or
futile attempts to galvanise the dead past.
The consequence is that the Atonement is
never preached.

' I met in August,' wrote one, ' the head of a
well-known public school, a man devout and
of high character. He said the Church had
lost its hold because it had no message as
years ago, when its message was that all are
sinners, and Christ had died for sinners. And
yet he could not accept that message himself
(though he feels the need of a Saviour), because he holds it is unjust for the Sinless to be
punished, or make satisfaction, or die instead
of the sinful. Even God, he holds, could not
do this, because it would violate His nature
of perfect holiness.'

And another wrote : ' I have been a
preacher between thirty and forty years. In
my young days the forensic theory of the
Atonement was the main burden of my

sermons. More mature thought, however, convinced me that the theory was unsound, and gradually it dropped out of my preaching. But there seemed nothing to put in its place. I bought Dr. Dale's book on the Atonement, but it seemed to say nothing in answer to the doubts that would arise in my mind. Since then, I fear, my sermons have been largely moral essays. I am more conscious than ever that the world needs a Saviour, and that Jesus Christ is the only One who can meet its need, and I long to be able adequately to present Him as such to those to whom I preach Sunday by Sunday. But I do not know how to present Him. I find the Bible full of the doctrine of the Atonement, but how is it to be interpreted? I notice that modern theology is almost wholly destructive. We need a positive and definite pronouncement on this great and vital question. I am very thankful for the hints you have so kindly given, but they are just enough to make me

long for more in the same direction. I am
sure that multitudes of my brethren are
waiting for an authoritative and definite
reply to these questions, and that, if it can
be given, it will be the fulcrum that Archi-
medes longed for.'

It is in response to such appeals that I have
written this book, indicating the pathway
which my own mind has travelled amid the
perplexities which the emergence of a new
intellectual order inevitably occasions. My
argument may indeed prove unconvincing,
but my purpose will be served if it stimulates
others to think out the problems with better
success. My interpretation of the infinite
truth may, and indeed must, be at the best
only partial ; yet this merit at least it possesses, that it has satisfied my own mind and
has brought others into ' the peace which
passeth all understanding.' It is the message
which, in the happy days of my own pulpit
ministry, I proclaimed with a glad heart and

ever clearer conviction ; and now that I have written it, my prayer is that it may still prove, by the grace of the Holy Spirit, ' the power of God unto salvation.'

D. S.

4 THE COLLEGE,
    LONDONDERRY.

CONTENTS

ATONEMENT AND EVOLUTION

ATONEMENT AND EVOLUTION

> ' A Fall of some sort or other—the creation, as
> it were, of a non-absolute—is the fundamental
> postulate of the moral history of man. Without
> this hypothesis, man is unintelligible; with it,
> every phenomenon is explicable. The mystery
> itself is too profound for human insight.'—
> S. T. COLERIDGE.

' ATONEMENT ' is a noble old English word. The term
'atonement.'
It signifies properly ' setting at one,' and hence
the removing of enmity and the healing of
estrangement ; and it was originally, like the
corresponding verb ' atone,' not a *verbum
sacrum* but a term of ordinary daily speech.
It was thus employed by Shakespeare :—

> ' Be assured, my good lord marshal,
> If we do now make our atonement well,
> Our peace will, like a broken limb united,
> Grow stronger for the breaking.' [1]

But already in Shakespeare's day it had
passed into religious use. King James's translators employed it constantly, in their version

[1] 2 *Henry IV*, IV. i. 220-3.

of the Old Testament Scriptures, of the sacrificial reconciliation of God and sinners, and thus the word was consecrated. It appears also in their version of the New Testament in a solitary instance : 'we joy in God through our Lord Jesus Christ, by whom we have now received the atonement.'   Here, however, the original term is not unique.   It is the same which is elsewhere in the Pauline Epistles rendered 'reconciliation' ; and it is well that the Revisers have, after Wycliffe's example,[1] so rendered it in this instance, all the more since, though the ideas nearly coincide, the word 'atonement' in the Old Testament version represents, as will appear in due course, quite another term in the original—that which appears in the English New Testament as 'propitiation.'

'Atonement' is thus a scriptural term, and it is a beautiful and fitting designation of our Saviour's work.   The idea is that man has been alienated from God, and our Lord's office is the healing of this fatal estrangement. The Gospel is 'the Word of Reconciliation.'

Rom. v. 11.

Its soteriological significance.

2 Cor. v. 19.

[1] Wycl. : 'we glorien in god by our lorde Jhesu crist : by whom we have receyvyde nowe the recounseylynge (or acordynge).'

It proclaims Redemption by Jesus Christ and Regeneration by the Holy Spirit, and it rests on the assumption of ruin by the Fall.

The fact of the Fall is indeed a fundamental and necessary postulate of the Christian Faith ; and here emerges an initial problem of extreme gravity. The modern theory of the universe is the evolutionary hypothesis, and it views the course of human history as a continuous and uninterrupted ascent. Man started as an animal, and he has gradually struggled upward to his present condition. Nor has he yet reached his goal ; for his development is still in progress, and there is no foreseeing what heights he may hereafter attain. His past history, however, is clearly legible. Animalism, savagery, civilisation— these are the successive stages of his long career. And this would seem to necessitate a profound modification of the Christian conception, especially in two particulars. First, there appears to be no longer any room for the idea of a primal apostasy. It is an unscientific fancy that man was created perfect and fell from that high estate. In truth he is nearer perfection now than he has ever

Evolution and the history of the race.

been. And again, 'sin' disappears. What theologians have so denominated is nothing abnormal. It is merely the natural and inevitable imperfection of an incomplete development, like the bitterness of unripe fruit ; and no remedy is required.

Is Redemption eliminated?

Hence it seems as though on the scientific theory of the universe the very idea of Redemption were eliminated. There was no Fall ; there is no sin ; and therefore there is no alienation from God. It follows that there is no Atonement. None is needed. Humanity is on the road to perfection, and it will in due season attain its goal by the normal process of development. This were indeed a cataclysmic *dénouement*, and no Christian soul could contemplate without dismay the destruction of that rich treasure which is the Church's agelong heritage—the Gospel of God's redeeming love and grace in our Lord Jesus Christ. Our present task is to consider the situation, and see whether, on the modern theory of the universe, there be not still room for the ancient faith ; whether indeed it be not more securely established.

And the first fact which emerges is that,

even if the utmost claim of science be allowed, the essence of Christianity is unimpaired. The Fall may be eliminated, but the Incarnation remains. It was an ancient *quæstio theologicalis* ' whether, if man had not sinned, God would have been incarnate ' : *Utrum, si homo non peccasset, Deus incarnatus fuisset ?* It presented itself at an early date, and it was invariably answered in the negative by the Fathers. They viewed the Incarnation as merely a remedial measure, the response of God's mercy to the need of sinful man ; and on this assumption it seemed to them self-evident that, had there been no sin, there would have been no Incarnation. 'Had flesh,' says St. Irenæus,[1] ' not needed saving, in no wise had the Word of God been made flesh.' ' The need of man,' says St. Athanasius,[2] ' precedes His becoming man, and apart from this He had not assumed flesh.' And so St. Augustine. Discoursing on that ' faithful saying ' of the Apostle : ' Christ Jesus came into the world to save sinners,' he

1. Permanence of the Incarnation.

An ancient question.

Patristic negation.

1 Tim. i. 15.

---

[1] v. xiv. 1.

[2] *Contra Arianos Oratio*, III. p. 424 D. (Coloniae, 1686) : προηγεῖται γὰρ τοῦ γενέσθαι αὐτὸν ἄνθρωπον ἡ τῶν ἀνθρώπων χρεία, ἧς ἄνευ οὐκ ἂν ἐνεδύσατο σάρκα.

argues : [1] ' There was no reason for the coming of Christ the Lord but to save sinners. Remove the disease, remove the wounds, and there is no reason for the medicine.'

Mediæval affirmation.

Such was the universal opinion of the Fathers, but it was challenged in the Middle Ages by Abelard, Alexander of Hales, Albertus Magnus, and others. It was recognised with growing clearness that, as St. Augustine had already observed,[2] ' there is much else in the Incarnation besides the remission of sins.' It was an eternal purpose of God, His perfect revelation, the supreme exaltation of humanity and the consummation of creation ; and therefore Christ would have come though man had never sinned. St. Thomas Aquinas inclined to this view in his early work on the *Sentences* of Peter the Lombard ;[3] but he reverted, though somewhat hesitatingly, to the patristic opinion in his *Summa Theologica.*[4]

Reformed affirmation.

Osiander.

At the Reformation the question was raised afresh, and the affirmative was maintained by Andreas Osiander, the Lutheran Professor of Theology at Königsberg (b. 1498, d. 1552).

[1] *Serm.* clxxv. 1.   [2] *De Trin.*, XIII. 22.
[3] III. i. 1. (3).   [4] III. i. 3.

His position was that 'even if man had not sinned, God had still become incarnate, though without being crucified,' *etiamsi homo non peccasset, Deus tamen incarnatus est, licet non crucifixus.* He was fiercely assailed by Calvin[1] and subsequently by Francis Turrettin, that stalwart protagonist of 'the Protestant scholastic';[2] nevertheless his doctrine held the field and has won general consent. The idea is that the Incarnation was no mere after-thought, no mere remedy necessitated by the accident of sin, but an eternal purpose of the Creator, the fulfilment of humanity's ideal, and the realisation of the essential unity of God and man. 'If,' says Bishop Martensen,[3] 'the Redeemer of the Martensen. world stands in an eternal relation to the Father and to humanity, if His person has not merely an historical, not merely a religious and ethical, but also a metaphysical significance, sin alone cannot have been the ground of His revelation ; for there was no metaphysical necessity for sin entering the world, and Christ would not be our Redeemer,

---

[1] *Instit.*, II. xii. 4, 5.   [2] *Instit. Theol.*, XIII. iii.
[3] *Chr. Dogm.*, pp. 260 ff.

if it had not been eternally involved in His idea that He should be our Mediator. Are we to suppose that the most glorious fact in the world was possible only through sin, and that apart from sin there would have been no place in history for the Only-begotten ? . . . If we recognise that quite apart from sin the union of humanity with God is involved in the idea of the perfection of the world, . . . we are led back to the Only-begotten, who appeared in the midst of the process of human development as the incarnation of the divine nature, as the beginner of the world's perfection, and as the personal manifestation and embodiment of the goal of God's ways with man.' And this is no mere speculation. It is the thought which St. Paul expresses when he says that Christ was ' the image of the invisible God, the first-born of all creation,' and we were ' created in Him for good works, which God afore prepared that we should walk in them.' The Eternal Son was the Archetype of humanity, and His manifestation in the flesh was the realisation of humanity's ideal. It was no redemptive after-thought, but an eternal purpose of the

Col. i. 15 ;
Eph. ii. 10.

Creator, and though man had never sinned, He would still have become incarnate.

And thus on the scientific theory the Incarnation remains. This is much, and it is not all ; for if only the scriptural representation be truly defined, it will appear that the idea of Redemption also still maintains its place. Here it is needful to recollect the distinction between *innocence* and *perfection*. Man, in the Pythagorean phrase, is ' a microcosm,' and the life of the individual is a miniature of the history of the race. It begins with childhood, and childhood is the age of innocence. It is not the age of perfection. This is the final stage, and it is attained by the long and painful discipline of the years. It is the fruit of experience, the crown of conflict. And the race also had its childhood, its age of innocence ; but that was only the beginning. The ordeal of history lay before it ; and the Creator's purpose was that humanity should grow from age to age toward the perfection of full manhood. This growth is, in scientific phrase, the evolution of the race, its unfolding like a seed, ' first the blade, then the ear, then the full corn.'

2. The primal state: *innocence*, not *perfection*.

Mk. iv. 28.

The Fall a departure from normal course of development.

The significant fact is that, according to the scriptural representation, when man fell, it was not from a state of perfection but from a state of innocence. As the Westminster Divines have expressed it : ' Our first parents being left to the freedom of their own will, through the temptation of Satan, transgressed the commandment of God in eating the forbidden fruit, and thereby fell from the estate of innocency wherein they were created.' In its primal state, the state of innocence, the race was in its infancy ; and it should, according to the Creator's purpose, have developed sweetly and harmoniously stage by stage until it realised its ideal and attained

Eph. iv. 13.

' unto a full-grown man, unto the measure of the stature of the fulness of Christ.' And the Fall was a departure from that course, an arrest of the normal process of moral and spiritual evolution.

Harmony of Scripture and Science.

It would indeed be foolish to discover in the scriptural narrative, adapted as it was to the mind of a primitive age, anticipations of modern thought ; nevertheless it is remarkable how accurately it conforms, in its broad outline, to the scientific account. Thus it is written that ' the Lord God formed man of Gen. ii. 7. the dust of the ground ' ; and Science reaffirms and amplifies this declaration when it teaches that

> ' All things the earth which fill
> Of but one stuff are spun,'

and our physical organism is composed of the common materials, the elementary substances —carbon, hydrogen, oxygen, and nitrogen. ' A fundamental unity of form and function underlies and pervades living matter from the slime of a stagnant ditch to the most complex animal ; the difference between living things being in degree, and not in kind.' [1] Scripture, be it observed, simply affirms the fact, and Science discovers the method, the long process of evolution whereby the Creator prepared a body for man. And then, when at length the body had been prepared for its habitation, the spirit was introduced into it. ' The Lord God formed man of the dust of the ground, and breathed into his nostrils the breath of life ; and man became a living soul.' It was then that the process of moral and spiritual evolution began ; and the Fall

[1] Clodd, *The Story of Creation*, p. 67.

was an arrest of that process, man's loss of innocence and his deflexion from the pathway toward perfection.

3. A theological supplement of the scientific theory.

It is here that the Christian and scientific views diverge. Science merely interprets the present facts, and therefore it recognises no antecedent disturbance of the orderly process of evolution. Thus far the Christian doctrine and the scientific theory agree, but at this point their alliance ends. They do not conflict ; they only part company. Science remains here, and Theology makes a farther advance and supplements Science by recognising the irruption of a perverting force which has dislocated the orderly process of the evolution of the human race and necessitated the remedial intervention of a Redeemer.

A legitimate hypothesis.

And the legitimacy of this affirmation appears when the limitation of scientific research is considered. Science takes cognisance simply of things as they are, and investigates their genesis and relations. Beyond this domain she cannot travel. The Scriptures affirm that at the outset of the evolution of the race there befell a catastrophe which has profoundly influenced its subsequent course ; and this affirmation Science is unqualified to dispute. She can only say : ' Of that I know nothing. It is merely things as they are that lie within my ken, and I cannot tell what may have preceded and determined the existing conditions.' [1]

An illustration is furnished by the history of Michelangelo's masterpiece, the colossal statue of David, which the Florentines used to call ' the Giant.' [2] It represents the young shepherd of Bethlehem facing the boastful Philistine, his sling round his back, his left hand on his shoulder holding the bag with the pebble, and his pendent right hand gripping the end of the cord, his figure poised just in act to hurl the missile to its mark. The story is that the marble had been blocked out in the Carrara quarry by a blundering sculptor, ' in such a manner that neither he nor any one else was capable of extracting a statue from the block, of the same size, or

The limitation of scientific investigation.

[1] *Cf.* Oswald Dykes, *The Divine Worker in Creation and Providence,* p. 5 : ' No more than this is the function of the sciences of nature. With the origin of things themselves, or with any purpose they may serve, or with their end-results, science as such takes nothing to do.'

[2] Symonds, *Life of Michelangelo Buonarroti,* I. p. 89 f.

even on a much smaller scale.' For a century it lay, apparently, a wasted mass, until
the master's eye detected its possibilities.
Its very mis-shapement served his design,
lending itself to the curve of the lithe body.
Now there are two authorities entitled to
pronounce on that supreme creation. One
is the art critic, and he considers its execution
and exhibits the method of the sculptor. The
other is the historian, and he speaks of the
accident which befell the shapeless block and
which determined the actual form of the
statue and altered the original design. Of
this the art critic knows nothing. 'I have
to do,' he says, ' simply with the statue as it
is ; and of that antecedent catastrophe I know
nothing. It lies beyond my ken, and I am
not qualified either to affirm or to deny it.'

The art critic corresponds to the man of
science and the historian to the theologian ;
and just as the historian is entitled, without
challenging the art critic's verdict on the
statue as it is, to recount the mishap which
has made it other than it might have been, so
it is open to the theologian, without intruding
into the domain of the man of science or im-

pugning his methods, to place at the beginning
of human history that disaster which is known
as the Fall and which has so potently influenced its subsequent course.   And the hypothesis is no mere arbitrary assumption.   It
is a necessary postulate, and it is established
by a twofold attestation.

A twofold
attestation :

There is, in the first place, the evidence of
the natural order.   In a universe otherwise
so harmoniously constituted the distempera-
ture of man's environment is plainly abnormal.   Science furnishes no explanation ; and
the only solution of the dark enigma is the
theological assurance that it is not an inherent defect in the cosmos but a dislocation
due to the intrusion of an alien force.   And
thus the doctrine of the Fall is a corollary
of the scientific axiom of the orderliness of
the universe.

(1) The order
of nature.

Then there is the testimony of the moral
instincts.   These proclaim that in his present
condition man is not merely an imperfect but
a fallen creature.   ' There is,' says Erskine of
Linlathen,[1] ' a deep melancholy in the highest
order of natural beauty, and a holiness.   It

(2) The moral
instincts.

[1] *Letters*, p. 83.

B

seems to recall the original state of man, and to reproach him, and yet to compassionate him for having lost it.' This is a profound thought. Why is it that the spectacle of a transcendent holiness rebukes us and excites within us an involuntary sense of shame? The reason is not merely that it reveals to us a perfection which we have not yet attained, for that would bring no reproach, but that it awakens in our breasts a dim remembrance of an innocence which was once ours and which we have forfeited. Display wealth to a beggar, and he will merely covet it. He will suffer no self-reproach. But take a spend-thrift to his ancestral estate, and show him the broad and teeming acres which are his birthright and which he has bartered away; and he will do more than covet these. He will blush for shame, and curse his ruinous folly. And even so the sense of guilt in man's breast is an instinctive confession that he is an outcast and an exile, fallen from his first estate.

HISTORIC PREPARATIONS

(1) THE MESSIANIC HOPE

'They all were looking for a king
    To slay their foes, and lift them high:
Thou cam'st a little baby thing
    That made a woman cry.'

GEORGE MACDONALD.

THE truth remains, unshaken by the progress The historic programme. of scientific investigation, that man is a sinner alienated from God, and an Atonement is his supreme need. And the satisfaction of this need was our Lord's paramount mission. He 'came into the world to save sinners.' All history had been a preparation for His Advent. Humanity had realised its sore need of reconciliation with God, and had been groping after it; and to Israel there had been vouchsafed a special grace, an ever fuller revelation of God, and an ever clearer vision of the Coming Redeemer. And thus, when He came, His work lay ready to His hand. It was prescribed by a twofold preparation.

The first was the Messianic Hope; and this The Messianic Hope. is the supreme miracle of Israel's divinely ordered history, constituting in truth her differentiation from the rest of the ancient nations. Their 'golden age' lay always in the past ; hers lay in the future, and she kept ever reaching forward in her darkest days to the promised glory. The Hope broke, like the dawn, dim at first but continually broadening from age to age unto the perfect day, ' the light of the knowledge of the glory of God in the face of Jesus Christ.' And here should be observed a significant fact, which has its counterpart in the development of the Christian interpretation of the Atonement— that, like all the revelations which were vouchsafed to Israel, the Messianic Hope grew out of the national experience, and it was shaped in each age by that age's thought. It was always God's response to His people's present need.

Its rise and progress.

Its earliest gleam appears in that passage felicitously entitled the *Protevangelium*, ' the First Gospel,' where it is written that after the primal Fall the Lord pronounced the serpent's doom : ' I will put enmity between thee and the woman, and between thy seed and her seed : it shall bruise thy head, and

1. The Prot-evangelium.

Gen. iii. 15.

thou shalt bruise its [1] heel.' Hard after the entrance of sin came the promise of deliverance, and it should be observed how meagre the promise was. The Christian Fathers and their successors interpreted ' the seed of the woman ' as Christ ; and the Romanists, following the mistranslation of the Latin Vulgate : ' she shall bruise thy head ' (*ipsa conteret caput tuum*), have taken it as prophetic of the Blessed Virgin. But neither reference is legitimate. ' The seed of the woman ' signifies merely her descendants, the human race. And thus the Protevangelium promises only *salvation*, not *a Saviour*. It is a prediction of the course which Redemption should pursue, and it is expressed in graphic imagery. Sin is likened to a serpent lurking by the path and fastening on the traveller's heel. It would be a sharp and painful conflict, but the issue was assured. Humanity, though sore stricken by the stealthy foe, would crush the serpent's head.

It was a far advance in the development of the Messianic Hope when it centred in a

2. The Prophet.

---

[1] Not 'his' (A.V., R.V.). The Hebrew word for 'seed' is masculine.

person, when the promise was no longer merely salvation but a Saviour. And this brighter vision broke in the days of Moses. ' The Lord thy God will raise up unto thee a Prophet from the midst of thee, of thy brethren, like unto me ; unto Him ye shall hearken.' The promise occurs in the course of Moses' parting counsels to the people whom he had led and disciplined so long. They had arrived at the frontier of the Promised Land, but he would never cross it. His work was done, and his departure was at hand ; and they would lack his presence and guidance in the new world which was opening before them. He perceived the perils which menaced them, especially the risk of contamination by heathen superstition. During their long pilgrimage in the wilderness they had been securely isolated, and he had been their prophet, God's spokesman, declaring to them His will and confirming them in His faith and fear ; but when they settled in Canaan, they would be encompassed by heathen neighbours and exposed to the seduction of heathen ideas. Bereft of their prophet, they would have no divine voice to guide them ; and in their

Dt. xviii. 15.

perplexities they would be prone to lend an ear to the impostures of divination, sooth-saying, and necromancy. And in view of this peril Moses assures them that God would be with them still and His voice would not be silent. The grace of prophecy would never cease from their midst, and it would culminate in the Advent of a Supreme Prophet who would be more to them than he had ever been. *Cf.* vers. 10-14.

Cf. Acts iii. 22.

Thus the Hope was shaped by the need of the hour, and the Messiah was pictured as a prophet. This ideal was soon thrust aside by others as the national life developed and fresh needs arose ; but it never quite perished. It survived vaguely in the days of the Fulfil-ment ; but these were degenerate days, and the Jews of that age exhibited this surest mark of decadence, that their eyes were turned backward. Inspiration had ceased, and tradition had succeeded. There was no vision of God, no living word. It was deemed incredible that a new prophet should arise, and the best hope was that the past might be restored. Hence the idea prevailed that ere the Messiah came one of the ancient prophets, probably the great Elijah, would The idea in our Lord's day.

Cf. Mal. iv. 5, 6.

return and herald His Advent. And thus
it is written that, when John the Baptist
appeared and stirred the nation with his
prophetic message, the Sanhedrin wondered
who he could be ; and two possibilities presented themselves to their minds. He might
actually be the Messiah, or he might be the
Messiah's herald. And so they sent deputies
to inquire. ' Who art thou ? ' they asked ;
and when he told them he was not the Messiah,
they inquired further if he were Elijah. This
also he denied. Perhaps, however, the
Messiah's forerunner would not be Elijah
but another of the ancient prophets ; and so,
exhausting every possibility, they asked :
' Art thou the Prophet ? ' [1]

*Jo. i. 19-21 ;
cf. vi. 14, vii.
40, 41.*

3. The King.   In the period of the kingdom again the
Messiah was pictured as a king, a scion of
David's royal lineage who should consummate
the nation's glory and make her the mistress
of the world. This conception found its
classic expression in that noble psalm which
has with good reason been recognised as the
prayer of David as his end approached for
his son and successor, Solomon, but which is

Ps. lxxii.

---

[1] Cf. *The Days of His Flesh*, pp. 27, 43.

at the same time a prophecy of One greater than Solomon. The Hebrew ideals were always transcendent visions of a glory beyond the range of human possibility. And thus they were never literally realised, yet they never missed their fulfilment. They were unconscious prophecies, reaching out blindly toward Him who should come and establish a nobler and diviner order. So it was with David's dream of Israel's glory under his successor : ' He shall have dominion from sea to sea, and from the river unto the ends of the earth. They that dwell in the wilderness shall bow before him ; and his enemies shall lick the dust. Yea, all kings shall fall down before him : all nations shall serve him. His name shall endure for ever ; his name shall be continued as long as the sun : and men shall be blessed in him : all nations shall call him blessed.' This glorious ideal was never realised by Solomon. Indeed his reign must have seemed a grim mockery of David's faith ; for it was the beginning of Israel's decadence. It ended in the disruption of the kingdom, and it was followed by centuries of ever-deepening disaster. Yet the psalmist's prophecy was fulfilled, and his dream was realised beyond his imagination in that King whose Kingdom is not of this world.

Degradation of the ideal.

Thus the seeming frustration of Israel's hope only enlarged it and carried it forward toward a nobler goal ; and in the dark days when the throne of David was tottering to its

Is. xi, xxxii.

fall, the prophet Isaiah proclaimed the advent of a King of David's house who should reign in righteousness and peace and glory. And to this hope the nation thenceforward clung. It was a noble ideal, but as the generations passed, it was grievously degraded. The national history was a succession of humiliations—the Babylonian captivity, the Greek invasion, and the Roman conquest ; and in their shame the Jews comforted themselves with the hope of their Coming King, and pictured Him as a national hero, like Judas Maccabæus, who should smite the heathen oppressor and strike his yoke from their necks. The Messianic salvation was conceived as a secular emancipation.

An obstacle to our Lord's recognition.

Such was the ideal which prevailed at our Lord's Advent ; and thus it came to pass that it was the Messianic Hope, which should have ensured His welcome, that constituted the chief embarrassment of His ministry and, more than aught else, turned the people's hearts away from Him. They were looking for a Saviour who could never come. They were dreaming of a king with a crown on his head and an army at his back ; and, with this ideal before them, how could they recognise their Saviour when He appeared ' meek and lowly in heart ' ? They would have laughed His Messiahship to scorn had they not *Cf.* Jo. vii. 31. witnessed His miracles ; and these persuaded them that He was indeed the Christ, and His lowliness was only a temporary disguise, and He would presently cast it aside and flash forth in His rightful majesty and ascend His throne. They fretted at His inexplicable procrastination ; and once, after the feeding Jo. vi. 15. of the five thousand, so convinced were they of His Messiahship that they attempted to seize Him and carry Him in triumph to Jerusalem and acclaim Him king. Even the Apostles shared the notion, and they were continually disputing which of them should be ' the greatest in the Kingdom '—which of them should be awarded the highest office and the richest emolument when He was seated on His throne. When the end came and they saw Him nailed to the Cross and laid in the sepulchre, they abandoned themselves to despair. 'We hoped,' was their lament, ' that it was He which should redeem Israel.' The Crucifixion crushed their fond hope; and when He was raised, it revived in their breasts, and they inquired if the time had now arrived for its fulfilment. ' Lord, dost Thou at this time restore the kingdom to Israel ? ' Nor was it until the Holy Spirit had been poured forth that they perceived the glory of the Cross and attained to the spiritual ideal of the Kingdom of Heaven. It is a tragic fact that it was their Messianic Hope that blinded the Jews to the Messiah's claims. They were cherishing a false expectation, and they did not recognise Him when He appeared. It was because He was the King of Israel that He was arraigned before Pontius Pilate on a charge of treason against the Emperor.

4. The Suffering Servant.

There was, however, another ideal, the noblest of all, which, though it had been obscured by that secular dream, still made its appeal to minds of a more spiritual order

Lk. xxiv. 21.

Acts i. 6.

Cf. Lk. xxiii. 2.

in these barren days. It had arisen amid the suffering and sorrow of the Babylonian Captivity. That heavy disaster was recognised as a divine judgment on the national sin; but the fact remained that there had always been a godly remnant, a faithful minority, who stood true to God and protested against the prevailing idolatry. And thus the problem presented itself: why they should share the national chastisement. The answer was that they were suffering not for their own sin but for the sin of their brethren. And hence emerged the profound thought of vicarious suffering and its redemptive efficacy. The Messianic Hope was cast in that mould, and the prophet of the Exile pictured the Coming Saviour as despised and rejected of men, Is, lii. 13-liii. a man of sorrows and acquainted with grief; bearing our griefs and carrying our sorrows; wounded for our transgressions and bruised for our iniquities; bearing the chastisement of our peace, that with His stripes we might be healed; and triumphing through humiliation. Though it was quickly forgotten, that was the deepest and truest of all the Messianic ideals; and it is the ideal which the Messiah came to fulfil.

(2) THE RITE OF SACRIFICE

' I know the anguish that is wrought
  Into the web of highest bliss ;
I know the Cross must be his lot
  Who thrills with Love's redeeming kiss.
But when the Lamb or Bullock fell
  'Neath the keen blade or shattering blow,
How that could make the sick heart well,
  Or nearer God—I do not know.'

WALTER C. SMITH.

A preparation for the Perfect Priest and the Perfect Sacrifice.

THE prophets of Israel were messengers of hope, ever pointing the nation forward to Him who should come. The priests, on the other hand, were messengers of mercy, and they were concerned primarily not with the future but with the present. They dealt with men as sinners, and showed them the way of reconciliation with God. Yet their office had also a forward look, inasmuch as its devices for bridging the gulf between God and man were all insufficient, and their very failure served to demonstrate the necessity of a better way. It was a preparation for the Perfect Priest and the Perfect Sacrifice.

The heart of the priestly preparation was the rite of sacrifice ; and the original idea of the rite was very naïve, befitting an immature stage in the development of humanity. The offering was conceived as the food of the deity. Thus in the Homeric poems the gods are represented as 'feasting on hecatombs,'[1] and in later Greek literature they bear such epithets as 'goat-eater,' 'ram-eater,' 'bull-eater.'[2] It was the savour of the sacrifice ascending to their nostrils that nourished them ;[3] and the notion is illustrated by the farcical proposal in the play of Aristophanes[4] that the birds should build a city in the air midway between earth and heaven, and starve the gods into subjection by refusing to let the savour of the altars pass unless they paid tribute.

Sacrifice originally an offering of food to the deity.

Israel started on the heathen level, and vestiges of this crude idea survive in the Old Testament literature, especially in primitive narratives like the story of the Flood, where it is written that ' Noah builded an altar unto the Lord . . . and offered burnt offerings. . . .

Old Testament vestiges of this idea.

Gen. viii. 20, 21.

[1] *Il.* IX. 535.
[2] αἰγοφάγος, κριοφάγος, ταυροφάγος.
[3] *Il.* I. 317.
[4] *Birds*, 187-93.

C

And the Lord smelled the sweet savour,' and in the stereotyped phraseology of the priestly ritual, where the offering is called ' the bread of God,' ' the food of the offering made by fire unto the Lord.'   In the progress of revelation, however, the idea of sacrifice was continually refined and spiritualised, and a psalmist of the prophetic order has put in the mouth of the Lord this protest against the heathenish conception :—

Lev. xxi. 8, 17 ; iii. 11.

Ps. l. 12-15.

' If I were hungry, I would not tell thee:
  for the world is Mine, and the fulness thereof.
Will I eat the flesh of bulls,
  or drink the blood of goats ?
Offer unto God the sacrifice of thanksgiving,
  and pay thy vows unto the Most High :
And call upon Me in the day of trouble ;
  I will deliver thee, and thou shalt glorify Me.'

Nevertheless, however it may have been refined, the initial idea persisted, that a sacrifice was a feast which God and the worshippers shared.   The offering was first presented to Him, and then they received their portions.   Thus it is written : ' And they brought in the Ark of the Lord, and set it in its place, in the midst of the tent that David

2 Sam. vi. 17-19.

had pitched for it : and David offered burnt offerings and peace offerings before the Lord. And when David had made an end of offering the burnt offering and the peace offerings, he blessed the people in the name of the Lord of Hosts.   And he dealt among all the people, even among the whole multitude of Israel, both to men and women, to every one a cake of bread, and a portion of flesh, and a cake of raisins.'

And it was this idea that constituted the atoning efficacy of sacrifice. A common meal bound the participants into one community. They were 'commensals'; they had eaten common food, and thus they had a common life. 'If I have eaten the smallest morsel of food with a man, I have nothing further to fear from him ; "there is salt between us," and he is bound not only to do me no harm, but to help and defend me as if I were his brother. So far was this principle carried by the old Arabs, that Zaid al-Khail, a famous warrior in the days of Mohammed, refused to slay a vagabond who carried off his camels, because the thief had surreptitiously drunk from his father's milk bowl

Hence the atoning efficacy of sacrifice.

before committing the theft. It does not indeed follow as a matter of course that because I have eaten once with a man I am permanently his friend, for the bond of union is conceived in a very realistic way, and strictly speaking lasts no longer than the food may be supposed to remain in my system. But the temporary bond is confirmed by repetition, and readily passes into a permanent tie confirmed by an oath. "There was a sworn alliance between the Liḥyān and the Moṣṭalic, they were wont to eat and drink together." This phrase of an Arab narrator supplies exactly what is wanted to define the significance of the sacrificial meal. The god and his worshippers are wont to eat and drink together, and by this token their fellowship is declared and sealed.' [1]

Vital efficacy of the blood.

The *raison d'être* of sacrifice was thus the establishment of a community of life between the deity and his worshippers ; and since the blood was the life, there was a peculiar efficacy in the blood of the victim. 'For the life of the flesh is in the blood : and I have given it to you upon the altar to make atone-

Cf. Gen. ix. 4.

[1] Robertson Smith, *The Religion of the Semites*, p. 252.

ment for your souls : for it is the blood that Lev. xvii. 11.
maketh atonement by reason of the life.' It
was recognised that the bond between the
deity and the worshipper would be most
direct and intimate if it were the worshipper's
own blood that was offered ; and this idea
appears in the story of the priests of Baal on
Mount Carmel. They first sacrificed a bul- 1 Ki. xviii. 28.
lock ; and when that offering evoked no
response, they resorted to a more efficacious
rite : they 'cried aloud, and cut themselves
with knives and lances, till the blood gushed
out upon them.' The ghastly notion persisted long, and so late as the beginning of the
Christian era it was the custom with certain
fierce and barbarous tribes that, when a
covenant was concluded, the parties should
drink each other's blood. Tacitus describes
the manner of the revolting rite among the
Parthians. 'It is the custom,' he says,[1]

[1] *Ann.* XII. 47. Æsop. *Fab.* 221 (Halm) is a curious
survival of this primitive idea in folklore. 'A man had
been bitten by a dog and was going about in search of one to
heal him. A man encountered him, and on learning what
he was after said: "Sir, if you wish to be made well, take a
piece of bread and smear it with the blood of your wound
and present it to the dog which bit you to eat." And he
laughed and said: "Why, if I do this, every dog in the
town will want to bite me."'

'for the kings, whenever they enter into alliance, to join their right hands and bind the thumbs together with a tight knot. Presently, when the blood has flowed to the extremities, they let it escape by a slight puncture, and lick it in turn. Such a covenant is held to have a mystic obligation as consecrated by the blood of both parties.'

Human sacrifice.

It was, however, only in a limited degree that the shedding of the worshipper's own blood was practicable ; and hence arose the horrid rite of human sacrifice. It was an especially Semitic institution, and it was practised to a late date by the Phœnicians and their kinsfolk the Carthaginians, and it would seem that, like many oriental superstitions, it was not unknown even in imperial Rome. At all events it was alleged that when Catiline pledged his fellow-conspirators, the oath was ratified by a draught of wine mingled with the blood of a murdered slave.[1] The idea of the rite was that, since the victim was akin to the worshippers, the offering of his blood established kinship between them and the deity. Hence it was reckoned speci-

[1] Sall. *Cat.* xxii ; Min. Fel. *Oct.* 30.

ally efficacious when the victim was the first-born of a noble house ; and there was rejoicing among the worshippers of Odin when the lot fell on their king.[1] And it is told how down to the reign of Tiberius mothers would bring their children and, soothing them lest their cries should offend the deity, would lay them in the brazen arms of the hateful idol of Moloch, to roll thence into a glowing furnace.[2]

Human sacrifice was practised by the Hebrews in early days, as appears from Abraham's purpose of offering his son Isaac on Mount Moriah. That story is not a prophecy of the Atonement ; it teaches not what sacrifice is but what it is not. It marks a moment in the evolution of religion, the discovery of a nobler conception of God and His requirements, though, as the story of Jephthah's daughter in the period of the Judges shows, the old conception was slow in dying out, being kept alive by the glamour of Baal-worship, and as late as the close of the seventh century it was necessary for a Hebrew

Among the primitive Hebrews.

Gen. xxii.

Jud. xi.

Cf. Mic. vi. 6-8.

---

[1] *Cf.* Trench's Hulsean Lectures, p. 219.
[2] Tert. *Apol.* 9 ; Min. Fel. *ibid.*

prophet to condemn the ghastly rite. It was banished from the national worship, and its appearance was always a recrudescence of heathenism. It was animal victims that were laid on the altars of Israel ; but the essential idea of sacrifice continued, especially that of the peculiar efficacy of the blood ; and the notion of the establishment thereby of a community of life between God and the people was expressed by its sprinkling first on the altar and then on the worshippers.

Cf. Ex. xxiv. 4-8.

No idea of atonement in primitive sacrifice.

The idea of atonement did not properly belong to the original conception of sacrifice. Indeed it was alien from the heathen mind ; for the heathen deities were immoral and capricious. They had no wrath against sin, and the purpose of their worshippers in bringing them offerings was merely to purchase their favour and conciliate their good will. They furnished the god with a savoury meal, and they expected that he would requite them by prospering their undertakings. And if he failed them, then they took to chiding him. Such was the frequent manner of the Homeric heroes,[1] and it persisted in more

[1] Cf. *Il.* III. 365, XII. 164, XIII. 631 ; *Od.* XX. 201.

civilised and enlightened days. Thus Plutarch
tells how, when Alexander the Great besieged
Tyre, a dream warned the citizens that their
god Apollo was displeased with them and
would go over to the enemy ; and, as if he
were a deserter taken in the act, they loaded
his image with chains and nailed it to its
pedestal, styling him ' an Alexandrist.'[1]
Even of the shrewd Emperor Augustus it is
recorded [2] that, when his fleet was wrecked by
a storm, he exclaimed that he would win the
victory in spite of Neptune, and decreed that
the image of the faithless god should be excluded from the next public procession. And
after a disaster to the Roman arms Julian
the Apostate burst into a passion and swore
that he would never again offer sacrifices to
Mars.[3]

Where such a conception of deity prevailed, A Hebrew
the idea of sacrifice as an atonement for sin development.
was impossible ; and it is the distinction of
Israel and an evidence of the peculiar providence which directed her national history
that her idea of sacrifice developed along
ethical and spiritual lines. It was determined

[1] *Alex.* 24.   [2] Suet. *Aug.* 16.   [3] Ammian. xxiv. 6.

by her conception of God. He was revealed to her as righteous and holy. He hated sin, and inasmuch as they were sinful, the people realised their alienation from Him ; and thus sacrifice became for them an act of repentance and consecration.

The sinner's pathway to God.

Jewish sacrifice, then, was an atonement for sin, dictated by the twofold consciousness of divine holiness and human guilt ; and its ritual covered the whole course of religious experience. It was the sinner's pathway to God, and it conducted him stage by stage from the alienation of sin to the peace of reconciliation. There were five stages in the progress, and each was marked by an appropriate offering.

Trespass Offering (Lev. vi. 1-7, vii. 1-10).

1. *The Trespass Offering.*—A ' trespass ' was a wrong done to one's neighbour ; and it is remarkable that the trespass offering is the first step toward reconciliation. The principle is that ere one can be right with God he must put himself right with his fellow-men, according to that precept of our Mt. v. 23, 24. Lord : ' If thou art offering thy gift at the altar, and there rememberest that thy brother hath aught against thee, leave there thy gift

before the altar, and go thy way, first be reconciled to thy brother, and then come and offer thy gift.' But a wrong to one's fellow man is also a wrong to God ; and therefore ' the law of the trespass offering ' is twofold : reparation of the wrong and a sacrifice to God. And the reparation must be not only full but overflowing, not merely exact restitution but ' restoration in full and the fifth part more thereto.'

2. *The Burnt Offering*.—This concerned a sin involving no trespass against one's neighbour—a sin against God alone ; and it required no restitution. It was an atonement ; it procured reconciliation.

Burnt Offering (Lev. vi. 8-13).

Cf. Lev. i. 2-4.

3. *The Meal Offering*.—This followed the sacrifice of atonement inasmuch as it was a thanksgiving for the forgiveness which the latter had procured. It consisted of fine flour and oil and frankincense ; and it was partly ' burned upon the altar for a sweet savour,' expressive of the worshipper's gratitude which ascended like fragrance to God ; and the remainder was eaten by the priests. It was a eucharistic sacrifice, and therefore none of it was appropriated by the

Meal Offering (Lev. vi. 14-23).

worshipper.   For gratitude renders ; it does not receive.

Sin Offering (Lev. vi. 24-30 ; *cf.* iv).

4. *The Sin Offering.*—This was a sacrifice for ' sins of ignorance ' ; and it was designed to meet the case of one who had done wrong unwittingly and then discovered it. His ignorance did not absolve him from guilt, since he should have known, and he would have known had he duly considered. An inadvertence evinces moral apathy.[1]   It involves guilt ; and therefore a ' sin of ignor-

Cf. Lev. vii. 7.   ance ' required the self-same sacrifice as a ' trespass.'

Peace Offering (Lev. vii. 11-34 ; cf. iii).

5. *The Peace Offering.*—This was a glad feast, celebrating the attainment of reconciliation, the consummation of the atonement.   The worshippers had won peace with God, and now they and God feasted in fellowship.   Both participated.   God's portion was

---

[1] The Greek term for 'a sin of ignorance' was ἀγνόημα (cf. Heb. ix. 7), and ἀγνοεῖν implied 'wilful ignorance,' ignorance due to inconsideration and therefore culpable. Cf. *Oxyrh. Pap.* 1188, 5 : στοχασάμενος τοῦ μηδὲν ἀγνοηθῆναι μηδὲ πρὸς χάριν οἰκονομηθῆναι, ὡς πρός σε τοῦ περὶ τῶν ἀγνοηθέντων ζητήματος ἐσομένου, 'making it your aim that there be no inadvertence or partial administration, since you will be answerable for inadvertences'—instruction to an official in making a valuation for purposes of taxation.

'.the inwards and the fat which is upon them ' ;
and this the priest burned upon the altar : it
was ' the food of the offering made by fire
unto the Lord.'   The rest of the sacrifice was
eaten by the worshippers—the victim's flesh
and unleavened cakes and wafers mingled
with oil.

Such were the successive stages of Jewish
atonement, the sacrificial pathway to peace
with God : reparation, forgiveness, thanksgiving, searching of heart, and the gladness
of reconciliation.   The ritual was a recognition of the guilt and misery of sin and the
sinner's sore need of deliverance ; and it was
co-extensive with his experience, providing
for every imaginable contingency.   Yet the
impressive fact is that it proved insufficient.
It met indeed the ordinary necessities, but
in the black straits of moral disaster the
sinner realised its impotence and craved an
adequate atonement.   So it happened with
the Psalmist when he had perceived the
enormity of his crime.   The priestly ritual
was efficacious for common need, but it was
unavailing for a case like his, and he knew
not whither to turn.   ' Thou delightest not

Insufficiency
of Jewish
sacrifice.

Ps. li. 16.

Heb. x. 4.

A prophecy
of the
True Sacrifice.
in sacrifice ; else would I give it : Thou hast no pleasure in burnt offering.' It was impossible that the blood of bulls and goats should take away a sin like his, and he longed for a better sacrifice. And this has been achieved.

> ' Not all the blood of beasts,
>   On Jewish altars slain,
>   Could give the guilty conscience peace,
>   Or wash away the stain.

> ' But Christ, the heavenly Lamb,
>   Takes all our sins away,
>   A sacrifice of nobler name
>   And richer blood then they.'

THE
PROBLEM OF THE ATONEMENT

THE PROBLEM OF THE ATONEMENT

' Our little systems have their day ;
  They have their day and cease to be :
  They are but broken lights of thee,
And thou, O Lord, art more than they.'

TENNYSON.

THUS, when our Lord came, He found His work defined by the course of the historic revelation. A double programme was presented to Him. He came to fulfil Israel's long dream of a Deliverer ; and so a ministry of vicarious suffering was His appointed portion. And He came also to satisfy her yearning after peace with God and achieve the reconciliation which she had vainly sought by the ritual of her blood-stained altars ; and so He was charged with a priestly office. He was the Perfect Priest, and His vicarious Passion was the Perfect Sacrifice ; and this is the problem of the Atonement : wherein lay the efficacy of His vicarious Passion, and how it achieved the reconciliation of humanity to God.

D

It should be observed at the outset that no definite and final solution of the problem is presented in the New Testament. It is indeed constantly and exultantly affirmed by the sacred writers that our Lord by His Cross has reconciled the world to God ; but they rest content with the affirmation and propound no theory. And if evidence hereof be required, it is afforded by the almost bewildering variety of theories which have been maintained by Christian teachers in the course of theological history, all diverse yet all claiming scriptural warrant and appealing to scriptural testimony. This would have been impossible had a precise and explicit doctrine ever been formulated by our Lord or His Apostles.

There are indeed several pregnant sayings of our Lord which demand recognition in the construction of an adequate doctrine of His atoning work ; but these are never formal or dogmatic : they are rather poetic and parabolic. And in truth it is in nowise surprising that He should have left the problem undefined and unresolved. ' My life,' said Henry Thoreau,

'My life is the poem I would have writ,
But I could not both live and utter it.'

And so, with all reverence, may it be said of our Lord that He could not at once accomplish the Atonement and interpret it. Only when it had been accomplished did its interpretation become possible ; and the latter task was reserved for His Apostles in after days when He was gone and the Holy Spirit had come in His room to guide them into all the truth.

Its interpretation the task of the Apostles.

And they performed the task ; yet the fact remains that they never formulated a precise, complete, and final doctrine. The Lord's atoning work was in their eyes an infinite revelation, exceeding the compass of the human intellect ; and each of them proclaimed only so much of the boundless wonder as he had been enabled to appropriate. Each approached it by the path of his personal experience, and found in it the satisfaction of his personal need. And thus it came to pass that each has his own conception of the supreme good which Christ has brought to mankind. To St. John the precious gift of the Gospel was Eternal Life ; to St. Paul it was Justification by Faith, the fulfilment of the Law's inexorable and infinite demand ; to

Variety of apostolic interpretations.

the author of the Epistle to the Hebrews it was Freedom of Access to God, ' boldness to enter into the Holiest by the blood of Jesus ' ; to St. James it was ' a royal law, the law of liberty ' ; to St. Peter it was ' a living hope by the resurrection of Jesus Christ from the dead.' Each of the sacred writers has his own theory of the Atonement, his own ' way of looking at it.' Each saw in Christ only so much as was revealed to him by the Holy Spirit, only so much as came home to him along the line of his personal experience and need. The Incarnation was an infinite revelation, and no human intellect, not even an inspired Apostle's, could comprehend it in all its fulness. And thus St. Paul confessed that he knew only in part and prophesied only in part. Each looked forth from his own window of the House of Faith on the broad landscape. Each had his own view, his own prospect ; but his vision was not all-embracing. There were other windows with different outlooks. Each view was true and wonderful, but none was complete, none included the entire landscape.

Thus the apostolic interpretation of the

Each moulded by personal experience.

1 Cor. xiii. 9.

Atonement was like the growth of the Messianic Hope. Just as Israel in each successive age had cast her ideal of the Coming Saviour in the mould of her national experience, so each of the Apostles found in Christ the satisfaction of his peculiar need. And this is the principle which has regulated the development of soteriological doctrine throughout the subsequent course of Christian history. Salvation is indeed a finished work, and the truth abides eternal ; but the truth is infinite, and the Church's knowledge of it has been a continual growth. Guided by the Holy Spirit, she has penetrated ever deeper into the ineffable mystery, and appropriated ever more of the inexhaustible treasures which are hidden in Christ. And the enlargement of her comprehension of the Saviour's work has always kept pace with the advancement of human knowledge. Each age has had its distinctive order of thought, and the dominant idea of each age has served as the norm of its soteriology.

And this fact prescribes the fitting manner of our investigation. First let us trace the history of the doctrine of the Atonement

Variety of historic interpretations.

Col. ii. 3.

Each moulded by the Spirit of the age.

The soteriological method.

and observe how each successive age has seen the transcendent mystery in the light of its master idea and fashioned its doctrine in this mould. And then, perhaps, it may be possible for us to prosecute the interpretation and present the eternal truth in the light of the fuller knowledge which is the Holy Spirit's gift to our generation.

Two mischievous tendencies :

It is indeed a difficult undertaking, yet it is most needful in these days when knowledge is so abundantly increased. It is a sacred duty which we owe to our Master and to the multitude of souls which would fain believe but are bewildered in a world where the old formulæ are no longer valid ; and there is a precept of His which it becomes His faithful ministers to heed in every generation, and not least in our own—that word which He spoke to the Twelve after a series of parables on the Kingdom of Heaven : ' Every scribe who hath been made a disciple to the Kingdom of Heaven,' that is, every true Christian teacher, ' is like unto a man that is a householder, which bringeth forth out of his treasure things new and old.' St. Chrysostom well illustrates the passage by referring to two

Mt. xiii. 52.

(1) Rejection of the new.

classes of teachers familiar in his day. One was the Jewish Rabbis. Their teaching was a slavish repetition of traditions, and no doctrine ever passed their lips without the preface 'Rabbi So-and-so says.' They brought forth out of their treasure only 'things old.' The other class was the Marcionite heretics. Marcion had held that there are two Gods—the Just God and the Good God ; and the former was the God of the Jews, while the latter was the Heavenly Father whom Jesus revealed. The Marcionites therefore rejected the Old Testament ; and so they brought forth out of their treasure only 'things new.' The true Christian teacher brings forth both. He retains the ancient faith, and he welcomes also the larger truth which is ever breaking from the Living Word.

(2) Impatience of the old.

These two tendencies are always at work, and there is constant need to remember our Lord's warning. God's truth is ever larger than our apprehension of it ; and the notion that even the best of interpretations is final is a denial of the continual ministry of the Holy Spirit whom our Lord sent at His

The continual ministry of the Holy Spirit.

departure to lead the Church ever deeper into His inexhaustible revelation of grace. Our attitude toward the fresh light which is now streaming in through so many opened windows, is a test of our faith. Impatience of the old is truly a fatal error; but it is no less fatal to cling obstinately to the old, reiterating ancient formulæ and banning larger definitions. The truth is a living growth, and a wise teacher will bring forth out of his treasure things new and things old—the old truth illumined and ennobled by the new light of God's Face, the Holy Spirit's clearer discovery of the Eternal Saviour. Here is the sacred office of a Christian teacher, never more needful than now—to bridge the gulf betwixt the generations, 'turning,' in the solemn words which close the Old Testament, 'the heart of the fathers to the children, and the heart of the children to their fathers, lest I come and smite the earth with a curse.'

The ages of Christian history.

There are, on a broad view, three ages of Christian history which have already run their course—the Patristic, the Mediæval, and the Post-Reformation. Each had its distinctive order of thought, and each cast its interpretation of the work of our Lord in that intellectual mould. And now we have entered upon a new age, the offspring of its predecessors and the heir of their spiritual treasures ; and the duty which devolves upon us in faithfulness at once to the past and to the future, is the interpretation of the ancient truth in terms of the new intellectual order. We are a link in the chain of the generations. We are runners in the torch-race, and our part is to carry forward the lamp of life and hand it on unquenched and undimmed. We are yesterday's heirs and the morrow's trustees, and we are charged to ' guard the deposit '[1] and transmit it not merely undiminished but augmented.

[1] τὴν παραθήκην φύλαξον (1 Tim. vi. 20).

HISTORIC INTERPRETATIONS

(1) THE RANSOM THEORY

' Sciendum est, ait, quod omnes doctores nostri
post Apostolos in hoc conveniunt, quod diabolus
dominium et potestatem habebat super hominem
et jure eum possidebat, ideo scilicet quod homo
ex libertate arbitrii quam habebat, sponte diabolo
consensit. Aiunt namque quod si quis aliquem
vicerit, victus jure victoris servus constituitur.
Ideo, inquit, sicut dicunt doctores, hac necessitate
incarnatus est Filius Dei, ut homo qui aliter
liberari non poterat, per mortem innocentis jure
liberaretur a jugo diaboli.'—ABELARD in ST.
BERNARD, *Epist.* cxc.

THE first of the Christian ages is the Patristic The Patristic Period : conflict between civilisation and barbarism.
Period. And its characteristic was the in-
cessant conflict between civilisation and
barbarism. The Roman Empire had established universal order, but in the remoter
regions unrest was still rife ; and the disturbing forces were brigandage and rebellion.
The mountains were infested by robbers, who
sallied forth from their fastnesses, and plun-
dered travellers, and held them to ransom;
and there was ceaseless commotion among
the subject tribes, and the victors demanded

ransom as the price of their prisoners' release.

The nightmare of captivity. The insecurity of life and property was a haunting nightmare, and one has only to read the literature of the period to realise what a terror it was. Two instances may serve to bring this home to our imaginations.

The brigands of the Taurus. Throughout the entire length of Asia Minor ran the great trade route, the artery of commerce between Ephesus and the Euphrates, and it was skirted to the south by the mountain ranges of Pisidia, Isauria, and Cilicia. Those wild fastnesses were infested by brigands, who were continually swooping down upon the caravans of merchantmen; insomuch that the Roman Senate planted a chain of fortified towns along the route for the protection of commerce—Antioch, Iconium, and Lystra, those towns which were the scene of St. Paul's activities during the first of his missionary journeys.[1]

[1] *Cf.* the incident which led to the suppression of the Cyprian monarchy by the Romans (Strabo, 684): Publius Claudius Pulcher, the enemy of Cicero and Cato, had fallen into the hands of the Cilician pirates and wrote to the king of Cyprus, asking him to send his ransom. The king sent money, but so little that the pirates refused it in disdain, and liberated Claudius without ransom.

Again, it is related that after the battle of Adrianople in the fourth century St. Ambrose, the Bishop of Milan, spent his all for the redemption of the captives ; and when that proved insufficient, he melted and coined the sacramental vessels, defending himself against the charge of sacrilege by the plea that the souls for which the Lord's blood had been shed, were more precious than the vessels which contained it.[1]

The thought of captivity was a haunting terror in that age, and the shadow of it appears already on the pages of the New Testament. Thus it is written in the Epistle to the Hebrews : ' Ye had compassion on them that were in bonds ' ; and again : ' Remember them that are in bonds, as bound with them ; them that are evil entreated, as being yourselves also in the body.' The reference here is to captives in the hands of their enemies or to exiles in days of persecution. The lot of these unfortunates was very grievous, whether they languished in prison or were set to toil in quarries, like St. John, according to tradition, in the island of Patmos ; and

[1] Ambros. *De Offic. Min.* II. xxviii.

the early Church constantly remembered their sore need and made mention of it in her intercessions. St. Ignatius charges the false teachers who were disturbing the churches of Asia Minor, with having ' no care for love, none for the widow, none for the orphan, none for the afflicted, none for the prisoner.' [1]   In his Epistle to the Corinthians [2] St. Clement of Rome prays : ' Save our afflicted ; pity the lowly ; raise the fallen ; manifest Thyself to the needy ; heal the ungodly ; restore the wanderers of Thy people ; ransom our captives.' And here is a petition in the Liturgy of St. Mark : ' Them that are holden in prisons or in mines or in exile or bitter bondage, pity them all, deliver them all.' And here is a similar petition in the Liturgy of St. James : ' Remember, O Lord, Christians at sea, on the road, among strangers, those in mines and tortures and bitter bondage, being our fathers and brethren.' [3]

Mould of contemporary soteriology.

Thus ever-present and distressful was the thought of captivity in that age, and it was natural that it should shape the contem-

[1] Ignat. *Smyrn.* vi.   [2] lix.
[3] Giles, *Cod. Apocryph. N. T.*, ii. pp. 636, 678.

porary doctrine of the Atonement. It lent a poignant significance to that saying of our Lord : ' The Son of Man came not to be Mt. xx. 28. ministered unto, but to minister, and to give His life a ransom for many,' and to its echoes in the apostolic writings. ' There is one 1 Tim. ii. 5, 6. God,' says St. Paul, ' one Mediator also between God and man, Himself man, Christ Jesus, who gave Himself a ransom for all.' ' Ye were redeemed,' says St. Peter, ' not with 1 Pet. i. 18. corruptible things, with silver or gold, . . . but with precious blood, as of a lamb without blemish and without spot, even the blood of Christ.'   Here is the mould in which that The Ransom Theory. age's doctrine of the Atonement was cast. Sin was conceived as bondage ; Christ was the Redeemer ; and His life was the ransom.

This is the Ransom Theory, and it is Abuse of the metaphor. indeed a beautiful and effective conception, but it was cruelly abused. ' How quickly,' says Thomas Fuller,[1] ' are mysteries made blasphemies when unskilful hands meddle with them ! '   The idea was poetry, and it was turned into dull prose.   The question was A ransom to the Devil. raised—to whom the ransom had been paid ;

[1] *Church Hist.*, ix.

E

and Origen answered that it had been paid to the Devil, the brigand who had taken us captive.   Here is his statement : [1] ' To whom did He " give His life a ransom for many " ? It was not to God.   Was it not then to the Evil One ?   For he was holding us fast until the ransom should be given him, even the life of Jesus ; being deceived with the idea that he could have dominion over it, and not seeing that he could not bear the torture involved in retaining it.'   The notion here is that the Devil miscalculated in the transaction.   He accepted Christ in lieu of sinful man, and he found his Captive too mighty for him.   He could not retain Him.   The ransom tortured him when he had it in his grasp, and he was compelled to relinquish it, thus losing both price and purchase.

(1) A mis-calculation by the Devil (Origen).

Ere long, however, it was recognised that on this construction the theory approximated perilously to Manichæism.   If it did not actually make the Devil a rival God, it at all events assigned him undue honour by permitting him to drive a bargain with God and exact a ransom from Him.   It was

(2) God's trickery of the Devil (Gregory of Nyssa).

[1] *In Ev. Matt.* xvi. 8.

accordingly revised by St. Gregory of Nyssa (A.D. 335-395),[1] who conceived that it was not a case of self-deception on the Devil's part. Rather the deception was practised upon him by God. The transaction was a trick. Sin was mankind's conquest by the Devil. He had gained the victory over them, and they were under his dominion ; and the Incarnation was a stratagem for their deliverance. Deceived by His seeming weakness in His state of humiliation, the Devil mistook Christ for a mere man, and would have usurped authority over Him ; and for this excess of privilege he justly forfeited his authority over mankind. The Incarnation was a device to outwit the Devil, and it succeeded. Some two centuries later the idea was picturesquely elaborated by St. Gregory the Great. The Incarnation, he taught,[2] was a divine stratagem to catch the Great Leviathan. The deity of Christ was the hook, and His flesh was the bait ; and when the bait was dangled before the Leviathan, he greedily swallowed it, and so

Gregory the Great.

---

[1] *Orat. Cat.* xv-xxvii.
[2] *Cf.* Dorner, *Syst. of Chr. Doct.*, IV. 12.

was taken. This crude and revolting theory persisted for generations ; and in the twelfth century it was expressed by Peter of Lombardy in a gruesome sentence : ' The Cross was a mouse-trap (*muscipula*) baited with the blood of Christ.' [1] This is the ultimate issue of the Ransom Theory, and it is surely soteriology's lowest depth of degradation.

Peter of Lombardy.

The Ransom Theory did not go unchallenged in the course of the Patristic Period, and its chief critics were St. Gregory of Nazianzus (A.D. 330-390) and St. John of Damascus, a monk of St. Sabas near Jerusalem, the last of the Greek Fathers and the greatest theologian of the Eastern Church, born at Damascus about the year 700 and surnamed for his eloquence ' Chrysorrhoas.' St. Gregory allowed that the Devil was the tyrant who held sinners in bondage, but he dismissed the idea that the ransom was paid to the Devil as ' a monstrous outrage,' since it implied not only that the brigand received a ransom from God but that God Himself was the ransom which he received. He perceived, however, a twofold difficulty in

Protests against the theory : Gregory of Nazianzus and John of Damascus.

[1] *Sent.* II. 19.

supposing that the ransom had been paid to God. On the one hand, how could it be paid to God when it was not God but the Devil that held us captive? And, on the other hand, how could the blood of His Only-begotten Son afford any pleasure to the Father who would not accept the sacrifice of Isaac but substituted a ram? He introduced the characteristically patristic notion of 'economy' or 'dispensation,' and argued obscurely that the Father received the ransom, not because He required it, but δι᾽ οἰκονομίαν, 'for a dispensational end.' It was an 'economic' transaction, and its true purpose was to bring about the Incarnation and the consequent sanctification of man.[1] St. John is no less emphatic in rejecting the idea that the ransom was paid to the Devil, but his account of the transaction is still more vague.[2]

Such protests indicate that even in the period of its ascendency the unsatisfactoriness of the doctrine was perceived, however dimly, and a more adequate interpretation desiderated. But none more adequate was forth-

St. Bernard's championship of it.

[1] *Orat.* xlii.   [2] III. 27.

coming meanwhile, and the Ransom Theory held the field until the twelfth century, when it was supplanted by St. Anselm. New ideas, however, win their way gradually, and the old doctrine still commanded the Church's faith more than a generation later. It was the doctrine of St. Bernard of Clairvaux (A.D. 1091-1153) ; and how he clung to it appears from the violence of his protests against Peter Abelard's denial of it,[1] though these, it should be considered, were exacerbated by personal animosity. Abelard admitted that the Ranson Theory had been the doctrine of all Christian teachers since the Apostles ; and it seemed to St. Bernard not merely arrogance but blasphemy, not merely temerity but impiety, that he should presume to challenge it. ' I hear the Prophets and Apostles,' he cries ; ' I obey the Gospel, but not the Gospel according to Peter. Are you founding for us a new Gospel ? The Church has no room for a fifth Evangelist. What else is the Gospel that the Law, the Prophets, the Apostles, and apostolic men preach to us, than what you alone deny, to

[1] Bern. *Epist.* cxc.

wit, that God became man that He might deliver man ? ' That was the significance of the theory to St. Bernard's mind, and its denial seemed to him a denial of Redemption ; and he assailed Abelard with the virulence which characterised theological controversy in that age and long afterwards. He was ' a man of perdition ' ; his doctrine was ' a lie.' ' Were it not more just that a mouth which talks such things should be beaten with cudgels than refuted with reasons ? '

It is painful to hear such language from lips which spoke so many gracious words and sang those hymns on the Love of Jesus still so precious to the Christian heart :— *His real concern the idea of Redemption.*

> ' Jesu dulcedo cordium,
> Fons vivus, lumen mentium,
> Excedens omne gaudium,
> Et omne desiderium.

> ' Nec lingua valet dicere,
> Nec litera exprimere :
> Expertus potest credere
> Quid sit Jesum diligere.'

The offence, however, ceases when the thought of the saint's heart is understood. The Ransom Theory expressed for him the Gospel of Redemption, and he was unconscious of its theological crudity.   Thus the rejection of the theory seemed to him a denial of the blessed truth.   ' You will not have it,' he said, ' that the Devil has or had power over man.   I confess neither would I.   Yet it does not follow that he has it not because you and I will not have it so.   If you do not confess or recognise it, they recognise and affirm it who have been redeemed by the Lord, " whom He hath redeemed from the hand of the enemy."   And this you would in nowise deny were you not under the hand of the enemy. You cannot render thanks with the redeemed, you who have not been redeemed.   For had you been redeemed, you would acknowledge the Redeemer and would not deny the Redeemer.   Nor does one seek the Redeemer who knows not himself a captive.'

St. Bernard's error lay in identifying the truth with a theory which was only a feeble attempt to express it ; and his attitude is a warning to believers in all ages, especially in times of transition when the intellectual order is changing and larger thoughts are emerging.   It is fatal then to cling to the old

Ps. cvii. 2.

A warning against identification of the truth with a theory.

definitions and persist, despite our Lord's admonition, in ' putting the new wine into Mk. ii. 22. the old wine-skins.'   The Ransom Theory was a valid interpretation of Redemption during the Patristic Period ; but when that period had passed and a new era had dawned with other institutions and ideas, another definition was needed, and the abandonment of the old theory was not a denial of the truth but its reaffirmation in larger and worthier terms.

(2) THE SATISFACTION THEORY

' Mine honour keeps the weather of my fate :
Life every man holds dear ; but the dear man
Holds honour far more precious-dear than life.'
SHAKESPEARE, *Troil. and Cress.*, v. iii. 26-28.

The Ransom Theory displaced by the mediæval spirit.

THE Ransom Theory of the Atonement is simply a flagrant example of the riding of a metaphor to death. In its later development it was shocking to the moral and religious instincts ; nevertheless, in spite of occasional protests, it held its ground throughout the Patristic Period, and it was displaced only by the advent of the Mediæval Period, bringing with it, as a new period always does, a new spirit which demanded new modes of expression and rendered the old formulæ no longer valid.

The Mediæval Period the age of chivalry.

Since each age has its peculiar and distinctive type of soteriological doctrine, shaped and coloured by contemporary circumstances and ideals, it was natural that during the Patristic Period, when war and brigandage disturbed the social order and oppressed men's

74

minds, our Lord's redemptive work should be cast in that mould. The Patristic Period passed, and the Mediæval Period succeeded. And what was the characteristic and dominant idea of the Mediæval Period ? It was the spirit of Chivalry, which manifested itself Chivalry. chiefly in the romance of knight-errantry and the high adventures of the Crusades. It made its appearance in the eleventh century and continued until the close of the four-teenth, but it survived far into the succeed-ing period in the practice of duelling. 'Chivalry,' says Buckle,[1] 'was to manners what feudalism was to politics' ; and like feudalism it was an essentially mediæval institution. Its distinctive notions were Its distinctive 'honour' and 'satisfaction.' An injury or an notions of 'honour' and insult was regarded as a stain upon a man's 'satisfaction.' honour, and it could only be wiped out by satisfaction. It was not accounted necessary that the satisfaction should be a precise resti-tution, an exact equivalent of the wrong.[2]

[1] *History of Civilisation*, II, chap. ii.

[2] Satisfaction was not payment ; and the difference is thus defined by Hugo Grotius (*Rivet. Apol. Discuss.*) : 'Solutio est, ubi id datur creditori quod in obligatione erat ; satisfactio, ubi aliud, sive par, sive majus, sive minus, volente creditore.'

An assertion of one's honour sufficed for its vindication. This appears, for example, in Sir Jasper Cranbourne's negotiation with Major Bridgenorth in presenting the latter with the challenge of Sir Geoffrey Peveril and offering him an opportunity to clear himself of the indignity which he had suffered : [1] ' I vow to Heaven, sir, that your honour lies a-bleeding ; and that in condescending to afford you this fair meeting, and thereby giving you some chance to stop its wounds, Sir Geoffrey has been moved by a tender sense of your condition, and an earnest wish to redeem your dishonour. And it will be but the crossing of your blade with his honoured sword for the space of some few minutes, and you will either live or die a noble and honoured gentleman ; besides that the knight's exquisite skill of fence may enable him, as his good nature will incline him, to disarm you with some flesh wound, little to the damage of your person, and greatly to the benefit of your reputation.'

The Satisfaction Theory.   Such was the institution of chivalry, and it is the mould in which the mediæval inter-

---

[1] Scott, *Peveril of the Peak*, chap. ix.

pretation of the Atonement was cast. That interpretation is the Satisfaction Theory, and it was formulated by the celebrated Archbishop of Canterbury, St. Anselm (b. 1033, d. 1109). His book *Cur Deus Homo ?* appeared in the year 1098. He had begun it in England, but when he finished it he was an exile in the province of Capua. It is incomparably the greatest of all works on the Atonement, and will always remain a theological classic, a splendid monument of sanctified intellectuality, and a precious contribution toward the solution of this sacred problem.

St. Anselm's Cur Deus Homo ?

It possesses this historic distinction, that it dealt the Ransom Theory its death-blow, not so much by its argument as by its recognition of the ideals of the new age and its interpretation of the thoughts which were stirring in men's minds. The argument is prefaced by a refutation of the decadent doctrine. The assumption of the latter is that the Devil was entitled in justice to receive a ransom for the liberation of mankind, since he had them in his possession, and it would have been an act of injustice had God effected

His refutation of the Ransom Theory.

their liberation by force.   Thus St. Bernard, in his attack on Abelard, quotes our Lord's words to Pilate, ' who was a limb of Satan ' : Jo. xix. 11. ' Thou wouldest have no power against Me, except it were given thee from above,' and argues : ' Nor, I think, will he plead that a power given from above was unjust. Let him therefore learn that the Devil had not only power but just power over men, so that he may consequently see this, that the Son of God surely came to deliver men.   But though we call the Devil's power just, we do not call his will so.   Whence not the Devil who made the assault, nor men who merited it, but the Lord who exposed him to it, is just.   For it is not from his power but from his will that one is called just or unjust.   Therefore a certain right of the Devil over man, though not acquired by right but wickedly usurped, was yet justly permitted.   So then man was justly held captive, yet so that the justice was neither in man nor in the Devil but in God.   Man therefore was justly given over but mercifully delivered ;   yet in such wise mercifully that there was not lacking a certain justice in the very deliverance, since this also concerned the Deliverer's mercy that He should rather employ justice against the assailant than power.' This St. Anselm denies. 'For,' he reasons,[1] 'if the Devil or man belonged to himself or to another than God, or remained in another power than God's, perhaps this were rightly said. But since the Devil or man is God's only and neither stands outside the power of God, what dealing was God bound to have with His own, concerning His own, in His own, save to punish His slave who had persuaded his fellow-slave to desert the common Master and come over to himself, and had traitorously received the run-away and thievishly received the thief with his theft from his Master ?'

Thus St. Anselm disposes of the old theory. *His own theory.* It is not sufficient, however, to refute a false theory unless one puts another and truer theory in its place ; and to this task he forthwith addresses himself. 'If,' he argues,[2] *Definition of Sin.* 'angel or man always rendered to God what he owes, he would never sin. Wherefore to sin is nothing else than not to render to God

[1] I. vii.   [2] I. xi.

what is owed (*non est itaque aliud peccare quam Deo non reddere debitum*).   Every will of a rational creature ought to be subject to the will of God.   This is the thing owed, which angel and man owe to God, by paying which no one sins, and which every one who does not pay, sins.   This is justice or rightness of will, which makes every man just or right in heart, that is, in will ; this is the sole and entire honour which we owe to God and which God requires of us.   This owed honour he who does not render to God, takes away from God what is His own and puts God out of His honour.   And this is to sin.'

Our debt to God subjection to His will.

Its refusal a dishonour to God.

Here a question arises : Why should not God simply overlook the dishonour done to Him, and forgive it freely without atonement ? He requires this of us in our dealings with our fellow-men ; and why should He not forgive freely, ' of His mercy alone, without any payment of the honour taken away from Him ' (*sola misericordia, sine omni solutione ablati sibi honoris*) ?

Free forgiveness by God impossible.

The reason, says St. Anselm, is that there is a difference between God and us.   He is the Ruler of the Universe, and He must not let

A blow to the moral government of the world.

His honour be dragged in the dust ; else a blow would be inflicted on the moral government of the world : it would be weakened and discredited.[1] ' When God enjoins us to forgive quite those who sin against us, it seems a contradiction that He should enjoin upon us what it is not fitting that He should do Himself.' But in fact ' there is no contradiction, inasmuch as God enjoins this upon us in order that we may not usurp what belongs to God alone. For it pertains to none to take vengeance save to Him who is Lord of all ; for, since earthly powers do this rightly, so does God Himself by whom for this very end they were ordained.'

Therefore, it is unfitting that God should forgive sins ' of His mercy alone, without any payment of the honour taken away from Him,' since ' nothing is less tolerable in the order of things than that a creature should take away from the Creator the honour owed and not pay what he takes away.' That is, an atonement is necessary in order that He may forgive sin without compromising His magisterial authority. His honour must be

Two ways of vindicating His magisterial authority : (1) punishment ; (2) satisfaction.

[1] I. xii.

F

vindicated. And there are only two possible
ways by which it can be vindicated. One
is that sin should be punished, and the other
is that satisfaction should be rendered. 'It
must needs be that satisfaction or punishment
follow every sin' (*necesse est ut omne peccatum
satisfactio aut pœna sequatur*).[1]

Satisfaction
our only
escape.

Thus it comes about that in satisfaction
lies our only hope of escape from punishment ;
and now the question arises how satisfaction
is possible.[2] Who shall render it ? 'Tell
me, then, what will you pay to God for your
sin ? You answer : Penitence, a heart con-
trite and humbled, manifold bodily labours,
mercy in giving and forgiving, and obedience.

Impossibility
of rendering it
ourselves.

But in all this what are you giving to God ?
When you render anything which you owe
even if you have not sinned, you ought not
to reckon this in lieu of the debt which you
owe for sin.' That is to say, there is no such
thing as superfluous or supererogatory merit.
The constant debt which we owe to God is
perfect obedience, and we can never render
a surplus obedience to make amends for past
failures. 'What, then, will you render to

[1] I. xv.   [2] I. xx.

God for your sin ? If you owe Him yourself and whatsoever you can even when you do not sin, you have nothing to render Him for sin. What, then, will become of you ? How can you be saved ? '

There is only one way.[1] You can be saved only through Christ. He must pay for your sin, and render the satisfaction which is the sole alternative to punishment. Outside of the Christian Faith satisfaction is not to be found. It is the work of Christ. He has rendered to God what is due to God and what sin has taken away from God—perfect obedience, complete subjection to His will.

Only Christ can render it.

Such in brief outline is St. Anselm's theory of the Atonement ; and it exhibits two important and distinctive features which merit consideration and remembrance.

Distinctive features of the theory :

One is the idea that Christ was not *punished* for man's sin. Punishment is the portion of the offender, and it was not and could not be inflicted on Christ. He was not punished : He made satisfaction ; He rendered to God such honour as vindicated His magisterial

1. Christ did not suffer the punishment of our sin ; He made satisfaction for it.

[1] I. xxv.

authority and made it possible for Him to forgo the punishment of sinners without compromising His authority or lowering His dignity in face of the universe. The alternative was *punishment or satisfaction*, and Christ rendered satisfaction that we might be absolved from punishment.

2. His life, not His death, avails.

And again, according to St. Anselm, the atoning efficacy lies not in our Lord's death but in His life. It was His obedience and submission to the will of God, maintained throughout the entire course of His days upon the earth, that honoured God and made satisfaction for man's disobedience. His death was merely the last incident of His life and the climax of His obedience.

Defects of the theory:

It will appear in due course that these are both principles of cardinal importance, essential to a true and scriptural doctrine of the Atonement. St. Anselm's is indeed a noble argument. It deals worthily with the sacred problem, and constitutes an abiding contribution toward its solution. In truth it merits the highest praise which a theory can win, inasmuch as it is nowhere positively erroneous. It is true so far as it reaches, and its insufficiency is due to the inevitable limitations of the age.

1. It is no trifling defect that the theory is unscriptural ; not indeed that it is contrary to the Holy Scriptures but that it is constructed apart from them and is not based upon their teaching.

1. Its independence of Scripture.

Nor could it be otherwise, since St. Anselm was a Scholastic and followed the method of the Scholastic Philosophy. That intellectual system was so named because it originated in the cathedral and cloister schools (*scholæ*), the forerunners of the Universities. It arose as early as the eighth century ; and it was an attempt, in nowise unsuccessful, to bring order out of chaos in the intellectual domain. Theology had degenerated into an unprofitable logomachy ; and the reason was that its authorities were the Scriptures and the ancient Fathers. Theologians appealed to these in support of their dogmas, and in this way there was no end of controversy. For ' proof-texts ' (*dicta probantia*) prove nothing. There has never been a dogma which did not allege scriptural sanction. In after days Protestants and Romanists, Calvinists and

Scholasticism.

Theological confusion.

Arminians all made their appeal to the common standard. The fault lay not with the Scriptures but with the unhistorical method of interpretation which prevailed ; and its futility was pithily expressed in the despairing epigram of the Calvinistic theologian, Samuel Werenfels, at the beginning of the eighteenth century :—

' This is a book where every man, whatever be his view,
Looks for a demonstration o't : looks for 't, and finds it too.' [1]

The Scholastic method. Scriptural and patristic citation was thus a hopeless method, issuing in endless and futile controversy ; and the Scholastics proposed to summon a third authority, a final arbiter. This was Reason. Where appeal to Scripture and the Fathers proved inconclusive, they would settle the controversy by dialectical processes. They were not ' rationalists ' in the modern sense ; for they believed the Christian doctrines. They accepted these on the authority of the Church, and they sought to ' add understanding to

[1] ' Hic liber est in quo quærit sua dogmata quisque ;
Invenit et pariter dogmata quisque sua.'

faith.' 'I do not try, O Lord,' says St. Anselm,[1] ' to penetrate Thy loftiness, for in nowise do I match my understanding therewith ; but I desire in some measure to understand Thy truth which my heart believes and loves. I do not seek to understand that I may believe, but I believe that I may understand.' And so, armed with the philosophy of Aristotle, who was to them as an inspired teacher,[2] they set themselves to the task of exhibiting the rationality of faith and the intellectual necessity of the Christian doctrines. Reason, they conceived, conducts inevitably to the goal which faith assumes. Leave revelation aside and explore the data of reason, and you find yourself confronted by the truths of revelation. ' As right order,' says St. Anselm again,[3] ' demands that we believe the deep things of the Christian Faith ere we presume to discuss them by reason, so it seems to me negligence if, after we have been confirmed in faith, we do not study to understand what we believe.'

[1] *Monologion*, i.
[2] St. Thomas Aquinas constantly appeals to 'the Philosopher' (*Philosophus*), that is, Aristotle.
[3] *Cur Deus Homo ?* I. ii.

St. Anselm's
method.

It is thus that he proceeds in his investigation of the problem of the Atonement. ' The first book,' he explains in his Preface to the *Cur Deus Homo ?* ' contains the objections of those who repudiate the Christian Faith because they think it contrary to reason, and the replies of believers ; and at last, putting Christ out of the question as though nothing were known about Him, it proves by necessary reasons that it is impossible for any man to be saved without Him.' Put the Scriptures out of account, he argues, and you find yourself driven back by the necessities of thought to recognition of the Incarnation and the Atonement.

Objections to
the Scholastic
method :

The Scholastic Philosophy was thus a magnificent *tour de force*, a high and courageous adventure of the human intellect ; yet its legitimacy is more than doubtful. Its basal assumption that the truths of revelation may be reached by the unaided processes of reason is nothing else than a denial of the necessity of revelation. It may be true that, given the truths of revelation, rational investigation attests them ; but it is very questionable whether, had these truths never been revealed, reason could ever have penetrated to them. In fact, until they were revealed, they never dawned upon the human intellect or were, at the most, only vaguely anticipated. And even if its legitimacy be allowed, the Scholastic method is open to grave objections, and not the least is that it turns the Gospel into a philosophy. It constructs Christian doctrine on a basis of pure reason, and its terms and ideas are both alien from the Christian revelation.

This appears especially in the Scholastic doctrine of the Atonement. Consider, for instance, that term 'satisfaction,' which is the kernel of the Anselmic theory. It was a good Latin word, and it frequently occurs in the Latin Vulgate, though never as a soteriological term.[1] And the Latin Fathers from Tertullian onward employ it in connection with forgiveness, but in their writings it is coloured by the prevailing Ransom Theory. At first indeed its soteriological

(1) Unchristian terminology.

---

[1] Cf. Mk. xv. 15: 'Pilatus autem volens populo satisfacere dimisit illis Barabbam et tradidit Jesum.' Acts xvii. 9: 'et accepta satisfactione a Jasone et ceteris dimiserunt eos,' I Pet. iii. 15: 'parati semper ad satisfactionem omni poscenti vos rationem de ea quæ in vobis est spe.'

use was somewhat vague. In St. Augustine, at all events, it denotes not Christ's payment of the sinner's ransom but the amends which the redeemed sinner makes for the past by penitence and devotion.[1] By and by, however, its soteriological significance was more clearly defined, and it denoted Christ's settlement of the Devil's claim by the payment of our ransom. The correlative term was the Low Latin ' forefaction ' or ' forfeiture.' Our lives were forfeited, and Christ's satisfaction was His payment of the forfeit by dying for us.[2] St. Anselm's use of the term to denote the satisfaction of God's violated honour was thus an innovation. It is alien from the Scriptures, and it was unknown to the Fathers. Indeed it was historically impossible during the Patristic Period, since it was a term of

---

[1] Cf. *Serm.* cccli. 12 : 'Non enim sufficit mores in melius commutare, et a factis malis recedere; nisi etiam de his quæ facta sunt satisfiat Deo per pœnitentiæ dolorem, per humilitatis gemitum, per contriti cordis sacrificium, cooperantibus eleemosynis.' *Enchir.* 19.

[2] Bern. *Epist.* cxc : 'Nam *si unus*, inquit, *pro omnibus mortuus est, ergo omnes mortui sunt :* ut videlicet satisfactio unius omnibus imputetur, sicut omnium peccata unus portavit : nec alter jam inveniatur qui forefecit, alter qui satisfecit : quia caput et corpus unus est Christus. Satisfecit ergo caput pro membris, Christus pro visceribus suis.'

Chivalry, and Chivalry was a mediæval institution.

Nor is it only in its terminology that the theory is unscriptural ; it is so also in its fundamental ideas, particularly its conception of God. It conceives Him as the Moral Governor of the world ; and while this is certainly a legitimate and useful conception, it is not the distinctively Christian conception of God. In the New Testament He is represented as standing to the children of men in a far more intimate and tender relationship. He appears there, and especially in the teaching of our Lord, not as the Moral Governor but as the Heavenly Father. This definition of God is the heart of the Christian revelation, and it will appear in the sequel that no theory of the Atonement which ignores it, is truly Christian.

(2) Unchristian conceptions.

2. There is another defect in St. Anselm's doctrine which is by no means peculiar to it but belongs to each of the historic theories of the Atonement and, as we shall see in due course, has been remedied only in recent days by the larger thought of modern Science. The defect is this—that the theory establishes

2. The satisfaction a transaction between God and Christ.

no vital nexus between Christ's redemptive
work and sinners. It represents Him as
making satisfaction to God for the violation
of His honour by rendering to Him the debt
which man owed and had withheld; but how
does this avail for man? It was Christ's
work, not man's; and how should it suffice
to absolve man from punishment?

Ne nexus
between Christ
and man.
St. Anselm never directly faces the problem,
and his nearest approach to a solution is an
affirmation of the oneness of Christ with the
race as the God-man. Only a God-man, he
argues, could make satisfaction for man's
sin, since, on the one hand, it could not be
made by one who was less than God, and, on
the other hand, unless he were also man, it
would not be man that made the satisfaction.[1]
'As it is right that man should make satisfaction for man's fault, so it is necessary that
he who makes satisfaction should be the
same as the sinner or of the same race; for
otherwise neither Adam nor his race would
make satisfaction for themselves.' But this
is insufficient. The question remains how
Christ was so related to sinners that His

[1] II. vi-viii.

obedience availed for them and served as a satisfaction for their sin.

St. Anselm's theory soon won acceptance. It displaced the decadent Ransom Theory, and it stands as the distinctive doctrine of the Middle Ages. Nevertheless it never obtained universal assent, nor was it suffered to establish itself without protest. Just as during the Patristic Period there were minds which were discontented with the Ransom Theory, so during the Mediæval Period there were minds which were displeased with the Satisfaction Theory and desired a more adequate interpretation of our Lord's redemptive work. The chief protest was raised by that brilliant though erratic thinker, Peter Abelard (b. 1079, d. 1142) ; and his doctrine of the Atonement is presented in his *Commentary on the Epistle to the Romans*, his *Theologia Christiana* (iv. 1308), and his *Sententiæ* (c. 23). It is nearly akin to the theory which was advocated last century by the American theologian, Horace Bushnell, in his noble and gracious work, *The Vicarious Sacrifice*, and which is commonly designated the Moral Power or Moral Influence Theory. Its essence is that the

A protest against the Satisfaction Theory: Abelard's theory of Moral Influence.

efficacy of Christ's work lies not in its influence upon God but in its influence upon man. The Incarnation, and especially the Passion, is a moving display of the Love of God, and it awakens a responsive love in our hearts ; and thus we are made righteous and reconciled to God.

St. Bernard's criticism.

The doctrine is indeed open to criticism, and it was bitterly censured by St. Bernard.[1] ' This,' he says after expounding what seemed to him the scriptural doctrine of Justification, ' is the righteousness of man in the Redeemer's blood, which a man of perdition, windy and sneering, endeavours so far to evacuate that all the Lord's emptying Himself of glory, His being made lower than the angels, His being born of a woman, His sojourning in the world, His experience of infirmities, His suffering of indignities, in fine, His return through the death of the Cross unto His own, he thinks and maintains must be reduced to this, that He delivered to men a type of life by living and teaching, and by suffering and dying fixed in their view the goal of charity. Did He, then, teach righteous-

[1] *Epist.* cxc.

ness and not give it, display charity but not infuse it, and so return unto His own ? ' It is easy thus to criticise the Moral Influence Theory, and that theory is indeed no adequate solution of the transcendent problem ; nevertheless it takes account of essential factors which the historic theories have neglected and which must find a place in a truly scriptural soteriology.

(3) THE FORENSIC THEORY

> ' Aristotle noted with his usual shrewdness of
> observation that the form of religion in a state
> generally follows with fair closeness that of its
> temporal government, so that men will be more
> inclined to believe in what the Greeks called
> " monarchy," or the active rule of One First Cause,
> if they live under a despot or absolute king
> than if they are members of a democracy.'—
> F. LEGGE.

The Post-
Reformation
Period. As we have seen, each successive period of
history has produced its peculiar type of
soteriological doctrine, cast in the mould of
its dominant conception. During the Patristic
Period brigandage and warfare prevailed,
and from this order of ideas sprang the Ransom
Theory of the Atonement. Sin was conceived
as bondage and salvation as redemption.
Mankind had been taken captive by the
Devil, and the life of Christ was their ransom,
the price paid to the enemy for their deliverance. The Mediæval Period, again, was the
age of Chivalry, and the Atonement was
interpreted in terms of that romantic in-

stitution. Sin was defined as a violation of God's 'honour' and Christ's work as a 'satisfaction.' And now we pass on to the third period—the period which was ushered in by the Reformation.

It should be observed that there is a marked difference between the Reformed doctrine and the doctrine of the Reformers. The Reformation was nothing else than an evangelical revival, and the Reformers were preachers rather than theologians. It was later, when the early enthusiasm had subsided and the inevitable period of reflection had succeeded, that the faith which had made a new Europe was reduced to an intellectual system—that stern and rigid system which was formulated by the Synod of Dort in 1618 and adopted by the Westminster Assembly in 1643. The Post-Reformation Period was, as it has been justly styled, the age of 'the Protestant Scholastic.' *The period of 'the Protestant Scholastic.'*

Now what was the distinctive order of thought which dominated that period and shaped its theological conceptions, particularly its doctrine of the Atonement? Just as the thought of the Patristic Period had been *Its dominant ideas:*

coloured by the horror of captivity and that
of the Mediæval Period by the romance of
Chivalry, so the Post-Reformation Period
was dominated by two contemporary ideas,
apparently diverse yet intimately related.
One was Absolute Monarchy and the other
Jurisprudence ; and it is remarkable how
potently they affected its theology. The
former was the mould which shaped its
conception of God, and His dealings with men
were expressed in terms of the latter. God
was conceived as the King, and earthly kings
as His representatives ; and here is the
reason of the servile homage and the worship-
ful titles accorded to royalty in that age.[1]
The King was ' the Lord's Anointed,' ' the
Vice-gerent of God upon earth ' ; he was
styled, as in the address to ' the Most High
and Mighty Prince James ' by his translators
of the Bible, ' Most dread Sovereign,' ' Your
Highness,' ' Your most Sacred Majesty ' ;
and to this day we speak of ' our gracious
King ' and ' His gracious commands.' Such
language would be properly employed only
of Deity, and the explanation of it is that

Absolute
Monarchy and
Jurisprudence.

[1] *Cf.* Buckle, *History of Civilisation*, II, chap. iv.

the King was regarded as God's earthly representative.

The unhappy consequence was that, in- *Rex Lex.* stead of requiring that the King should resemble God and condemning him when he departed from that ideal, men rather construed God in terms of earthly kingship ; and, since the King was an absolute ruler, superior to the law—*exlex*, as the phrase was,—they conceived God after this fashion. The question ' whether the King be above the Law, or no,' was keenly debated in Scotland during the seventeenth century ; and it strikingly evinces how deeply rooted was the theory of ' Divine Right ' that, when Samuel Rutherfurd published his famous book *Lex Rex*, with its sub-title ' A Dispute for the Just Prerogative of King and People,' maintaining that the right of the King is a fiduciary right, that he is the trustee of the people whom God, by their own choice, has committed to him, and that he is in trust to administer the law, not to break it, nor to dispense with it, the author narrowly escaped and the book itself did not escape the hands of the common hangman. Rutherfurd was cited before the

Parliament on a charge of high treason in 1661 ; but he was lying on his deathbed when the citation reached him, and he answered : ' I behove to obey my first summons.'

> ' They 've summoned me before them,
>   But there I may not come,—
> My Lord says " Come up hither,"
>   My Lord says " Welcome home ! "
> My kingly King, at His white throne,
>   My presence doth command,
> Where glory, glory dwelleth
>   In Immanuel's land.'

The mould of contemporary theology.

God was the King ; and since the King was the Law—*Rex Lex*, not *Lex Rex*,—it was inevitable that God's dealings with men should be legally construed in terms of arbitrary despotism. It is not a little remarkable how many of the theologians of that period were jurists, like the celebrated Arminian, Hugo Grotius (1583-1645). Perhaps the reason may have been, in part at all events, that Holland was then the home of theology, and the instinct for precision so characteristic of the Dutch intellect inclined it to the methods of the law-courts. The Dutch taste appears in the

Dutch gardens, so geometrical and artificial ;
and it made of theology much what it made
of horticulture.

The Reformed Theology was Dutch, and The Forensic Theory.
hence it was ruled by the methods and cast
in the mould of jurisprudence ; and nowhere
is this more apparent than in its soteriology.
Its doctrine of the Atonement is ' the Forensic
Theory,' and it is conceived in the spirit of
legality. According to its definition, God
is at once King, Lawgiver, and Judge ; sin
is a violation of His law ; and sinners are
criminals and traitors. And, in correspond-
ence with this definition, the Atonement is a
device for exempting sinners from the punishment which is their due without interfering
with the inexorable course of justice. The
expedient is Substitution (*subrogatio*). The
punishment had to be inflicted, and Christ
offered Himself as a substitute for sinners
and suffered it in their stead. As the old
rhyme puts it :—

> ' He knew how wicked man had been ;
> He knew that God must punish sin ;
> So out of pity Jesus said
> He 'd bear the punishment instead.'

The keyword of the theory is 'substitution,' just as that of the Patristic Theory is 'ransom' and that of the Mediæval Theory 'satisfaction.'

Difference between the Forensic Theory and its predecessors.

Such is the Forensic Theory, and it may serve to define it more clearly if we observe wherein precisely it differs from its predecessors. It differs from the Ransom Theory in this—that, while it also speaks of a ransom for the release of sinners, it represents the ransom as paid not to the Devil but to God. In the Post-Reformation soteriology God plays the part which the Devil had played in the Patristic. Again, it differs from the Satisfaction Theory in this—that, whereas the latter laid down as the alternative consequent upon sin 'either punishment or satisfaction' and represented Christ as rendering the latter on our behalf, the Forensic Theory conceives Him as choosing the other course and bearing in our stead the punishment which was our due. It employs the old term 'satisfaction,' but not in the old sense. According to St. Anselm, it was a satisfaction to God's *honour*; according to the Post-Reformation doctrine, it was a satisfaction to His *justice*.[1]

This, then, is the Post-Reformation doctrine of the Atonement. The work of Christ was a vicarious endurance of the punishment which our sin had deserved and which should have been inflicted upon us. We lay, by reason of our sin both original and actual, under the wrath and curse of God, sentenced to an eternity of torment ; and the doom would have been executed upon us had not Christ offered Himself in our room and suffered in our stead the stroke of God's wrath, and thus satisfied His justice and appeased His anger.[2] It is an unspeakably awful theory, and it has been expressed with uncompromising

An awful doctrine.

---

[1] *Cf.* Turrettin, *Instit. Theol.* XIV. x. iii : ' *Satisfactio* de qua hic quæritur, non sumitur *latè* pro simplici et qualicunque *offensae reparatione*, quum aliquis se purgat et excusat apud eum, qui offensam aliquam passus est. Sed strictè pro *solutione debiti*, qua solvitur quod alius debet, et qua satisfit Creditori, vel Judici, debitum, vel pœnam repetenti.'

[2] *Cf.* Turrettin, *ibid.* vi, vii : Sin (*peccatum*) is (1) a debt (*debitum*), (2) enmity (*inimicitia*), and (3) a crime (*crimen*) : ' Unde colligitur tria ad Redemptionem fuisse requisita ; ut debitum peccati solveretur, ut odium Dei et ira placaretur, et ut reatus expiaretur.' Correspondingly, Satisfaction is (1) *debiti solutio*, (2) *iræ divinæ placatio*, and (3) *reatus expiatio*.

severity in the familiar verses of the gracious
and saintly Mrs. Cousin :—

' Jehovah lifted up His rod ;
　O Christ, it fell on Thee !
Thou wast sore stricken of Thy God ;
　There 's not one stroke for me.
　　Thy tears, Thy blood,
　　Beneath it flowed :
　Thy bruising healeth me.

' Jehovah bade His sword awake ;
　O Christ, it woke 'gainst Thee !
Thy blood the flaming blade must slake,
　Thy heart its sheath must be,
　　All for my sake,
　　My peace to make :
　Now sleeps that sword for me.'

Nor is hers the only devout and tender soul
that has embraced the stern doctrine ; but
this, be it observed, constitutes no argument
on its behalf. For so long as a doctrine
remains unchallenged, faith feeds upon it,
extracting sweetness from its very bitterness.
Did not St. Bernard rejoice in the Ransom
Theory, repulsive as it now appears to the
moral and religious sense, and refuse to let
it go ? In truth it was not the theory that

he loved, but the Gospel of Redemption which it so crudely expressed.

The Forensic Theory is indeed an awe-inspiring doctrine, affrighting and oppressing the heart ; yet it possesses this conspicuous merit, that it emphasises at least two essential truths which the Holy Scriptures proclaim and which must be included in the formulation of an adequate theory of the Atonement. One is the terribleness of sin, its heinousness in God's sight, and the curse which it entails by alienating the soul from God and excluding it from His fellowship. And the other is the vicariousness of our Lord's work. He achieved our salvation by bearing our sin and suffering for our sake. His Atonement was a vicarious sacrifice. Both these truths are clearly written on the pages of the New Testament, and they are attested, moreover, by conscience and experience ; and it is mainly because it has taken adequate account of them that the Forensic Theory has exerted so potent an influence.

Nevertheless it is open to very grave objections ; and more and more, as the old order of thought which shaped it passes away

Essential truths :

(1) The curse of sin.

(2) The vicariousness of our Lord's work.

Grave objections :

and a new order is created by the ever changing spirit of the world, its insufficiency is being recognised and a restatement of the infinite truth of the Atonement demanded.

1. Breach between God and Christ.

1. The theory stands in direct and open contradiction to the fundamental article of the Christian faith, that Christ is one with God—one in character and purpose and disposition toward the children of men. It places a gulf between God and Christ, representing God as the stern Judge who insisted on the execution of justice, and Christ as the pitiful Saviour who interposed and satisfied His legal demand and appeased His righteous wrath. They are not one either in their attitudes toward sinners or in the parts which they play. God is propitiated, Christ propitiates; God inflicts the punishment, Christ suffers it; God exacts the debt, Christ pays it. This is the fundamental postulate of the theory. God and Christ are not one in character or purpose or disposition toward sinners; and what follows? Since Christ is different from God, He is necessarily less than God. And thus, when carried to its logical conclusion, the Forensic Theory issues

in Unitarianism. Nor is this an unpractical or merely theoretical contingency ; for it is an historical fact that it was from Calvinistic Presbyterianism that English Unitarianism sprang.

2. The theory proceeds upon an unreason-able and indeed unthinkable assumption, namely, that Christ endured the wrath of God in our room. It is indeed conceivable that He should have endured the punishment which is our due ; but that He endured the wrath of God in our stead is an unthinkable proposition. Punishment is transferable, but wrath is not. It is unimaginable that God should have resolved : ' I will withdraw My wrath from guilty sinners, and I will be angry with My innocent Son instead.' The notion is a palpable absurdity ; and though his successors in the period of the Protestant Scholastic, blinded by dogmatic prepossession, acquiesced in it, Calvin in the evangelical atmosphere of Reformation days recognised its irrationality and emphatically, though with questionable consistency, repudiated it. ' We do not,' he says,[1] ' suggest that God was

2. An un-reasonable assumption.

Transference of wrath unthinkable.

[1] *Instit.* II. xvi. 11.

ever His adversary or angry with Him. For
how should He be angry with His Beloved
Son in whom His mind rested ? Or how
should Christ by His intercession placate to
others the Father whom He had at enmity
with Himself ? ' [1]

Transference
of punishment
an illegality.

And further, while it is indeed conceivable
that God should have transferred to Christ
the punishment which belonged to sinners,
such a procedure would have been legally
indefensible. Bring it to the touchstone of
fact, and this will appear. Consider two

Examples :
(1) George Fox
in Doomsdale.

practical instances. One is an incident which
George Fox relates in his *Journal*. He was
lying in the filthy dungeon of Doomsdale at
Lancaster and, he says, ' a friend went to
Oliver Cromwell and offered himself, body
for body, to lie in Doomsdale in my stead,
if he would take him and let me have liberty.
Which thing so struck him that he said to his
great men and council, " which of you would
do as much for me, if I were in the same condition ? " And though he did not accept of
the friend's offer, but said he could not do

[1] Regarding our Lord's dereliction on the Cross (Mt. xxvii.
46) cf. my *Christian Counsel*, pp. 149 ff.

it, for that it was contrary to law, yet the truth thereby came mightily over him.'

The other instance is the offer of the Highland clansman, Evan Maccombich, when his chieftain, Fergus MacIvor, Vich Ian Vohr, was sentenced at Carlisle in ' the '45.'[1] ' " I was only ganging to say, my lord," said Evan, in what he meant to be an insinuating manner, " that if your excellent honour and the honourable Court would let Vich Ian Vohr go free just this once, and let him gae back to France, and no to trouble King George's government again, that ony six o' the very best of his clan will be willing to be justified in his stead ; and if you 'll just let me gae down to Glennaquoich, I 'll fetch them up to ye mysell, to head or hang, and you may begin wi' me the very first man."

' Notwithstanding the solemnity of the occasion, a sort of laugh was heard in the court at the extraordinary nature of the proposal. The Judge checked this indecency, and Evan, looking sternly around, when the murmur abated, " If the Saxon gentlemen are laughing," he said, " because a poor man, such

(2) Evan Maccombich and Fergus MacIvor.

[1] Scott, *Waverley*, chap. lxviii.

as me, thinks my life, or the life of six of my degree, is worth that of Vich Ian Vohr, it's like enough they may be very right ; but if they laugh because they think I would not keep my word and come back to redeem him, I can tell them they ken neither the heart of a Hielandman nor the honour of a gentleman."

'There was no farther inclination to laugh among the audience, and a dead silence ensued.'

A legal theory based on an illegality.

Such a transference of punishment could never be sanctioned by a judge.[1]   It would, as Cromwell pronounced, be 'contrary to law.'   Yet it is precisely such an arrangement that is involved in the Forensic Theory.   And here lies the peculiar irony of the case, that, while the theory interprets the Atonement in terms of jurisprudence, it bases it upon a flagrant illegality.

3. Unscripturalness of the Forensic Theory.

3. The Forensic Theory is fundamentally unscriptural.   It is radically opposed to the teaching of the New Testament in its con-

---

[1] *Cf.* Grot. *De Satisfact. Chr.* II : 'Talis qui sit Judex is nocentem non posset a pœna liberare etiam pœnam in alterum transferendo : non quia id per se injustum sit, sed quia legi non congruat, cujus ipse minister electus est.'

ception alike of God's attitude to sinners and of the *raison d'être* of Christ's work.

Consider, for instance, its use of the term 'reconciliation.' The theory represents Christ as 'reconciling God to sinners'; and this is precisely the reverse of the New Testament representation. 'Reconciliation' is a Pauline term, and, with a persistence and precision which evince conscious and deliberate intention, the Apostle constantly affirms that Christ 'reconciled the world to God,' never that He 'reconciled God to the world.' This is the *usus loquendi*, and it is invariably observed. 'If, while we were enemies, we were reconciled to God through the death of His Son, much more, being reconciled, shall we be saved through His life.' 'All things are of God, who reconciled us to Himself through Christ, and gave unto us the ministry of reconciliation; to wit, that God was in Christ reconciling the world unto Himself . . . We beseech you on behalf of Christ, be ye reconciled to God.' 'He is our peace, who made both one . . ., that He . . . might reconcile them both in one body unto God through the Cross, having

The term 're-conciliation.'

Rom. v. 10.

2 Cor. v. 18-20.

Eph. ii. 14-16.

Col. i. 19-21.

slain the enmity thereby.' ' It was the good pleasure of the Father . . . through Him to reconcile all things unto Himself, having made peace through the blood of His Cross. . . . And you, being in time past alienated and enemies in your mind in your evil works, yet now hath He reconciled in the body of His flesh through death.'[1]

Two essential truths.

Such is the Pauline definition of ' reconciliation ' ; and it involves two truths which are essential elements of a scriptural doctrine of the Atonement, and which the Forensic Theory not merely ignores but necessarily denies. One is that *the enmity is all on our side*. It is we that need to be reconciled to God, not God that needs to be reconciled to us. And the other is that *reconciliation is God's work*, and He accomplishes it through Christ. ' God was in Christ reconciling the

---

[1] The term 'reconcile' (καταλλάσσειν, ἀποκαταλλάσσειν) is employed in the New Testament exclusively in relation to God ; and it is significant that διαλλάσσειν is the word in the solitary instance where reconciliation between estranged men is in question (Mt. v. 24: διαλλάγηθι τῷ ἀδελφῷ σου). διαλλάσσειν implies that the enmity is *mutual*, but even here it is the wrongdoer that 'is reconciled' ('If thou rememberest that thy brother hath aught against thee, first be reconciled to thy brother'). On the Christian view one who needs to be reconciled is *ipso facto* a wrongdoer. Enmity is sin.

world unto Himself.' God and Christ are here one—one in spirit and thought and action.

These two truths constitute the basis of a scriptural and truly Christian doctrine of the Atonement. They are proclaimed on every page of the New Testament ; and it is worthy of observation that, though hidden from the Post-Reformation theologians by dogmatic accretions, they shone before the eyes of St. Augustine, and he repeatedly affirms them. ' Incomprehensible,' he says in one place,[1] ' is the love wherewith God loves us, nor is it mutable. For not from the time when we were reconciled to Him through the blood of His Son did He begin to love us ; but before the foundation of the world He loved us, that with His Only-begotten we too might be His sons, ere we had any being. Therefore the statement that " we were reconciled to God by the death of His Son," let it not be so heard, let it not be so received, as though His Son therefore reconciled us to Him that He might now begin to love those whom He had hated, even as one

Affirmed by St. Augustine.

[1] *In Joan. Ev. Tract.* cx. 6.

H

enemy is reconciled to another that they may again be friends, and that they may love each other who had hated each other. No, He already loved us, and we were reconciled to One with whom by reason of sin we had enmities. And whether I speak truly here, let the Apostle attest. "God," he says, "commendeth His own love toward us, in that, while we were yet sinners, Christ died for us." Therefore He had charity toward us even while, in the exercise of enmities against Him, we were working iniquity.' And again[1] : 'What is the meaning of "reconciled through the death of His Son"? Is it really so that, when God was angry with us, He saw the death of His Son for us and was placated to us? Why, then, was His Son already placated to us so far that He even deigned to die for us, while the Father was still angry with us so far that, unless His Son died for us, He would not be placated? And what means it that in another passage the self-same Doctor of the Gentiles says : "What, then, shall we say to these things? If God be for us, who is against us? He who spared not His own

Rom. v. 8.

Rom. v. 10.

viii. 31, 32.

[1] *De Trin.* xiii. 15.

Son but delivered Him up for us all, how hath He not also with Him freely given us all things ? " Why, unless the Father had already been placated, would He, not sparing His own Son, deliver Him up for us ? Does it not seem as though the one sentence were contrary to the other ? In the one the Son died for us and the Father is reconciled to us through His death ; while in the other, as though the Father were the first to love us, it is He that on our account spares not the Son, it is He that for us delivers Him up to death. But I see that the Father loved us even before, not only before the Son died for us but before He founded the world, on the testimony of the Apostle himself who says " as He hath Eph. i. 4. chosen us in Him before the foundation of the world." Nor was the Son, when the Father spared Him not, delivered up for us as it were against His will, since of Him too it is said " who loved me and delivered Him- Gal. ii. 20. self up for me." At once therefore the Father and the Son and Spirit of both work all things equally and accordantly.'

As we have seen, even in the days when they were the accepted doctrines of the

Atonement, neither the Ransom Theory nor the Satisfaction Theory went unchallenged. There were minds which recognised their insufficiency and desired a truer and worthier interpretation, dimly anticipating the larger thought of a new age yet unborn. And so it happened also in the case of the Forensic Theory. The chief protest was raised by that large-hearted and devout Dutch scholar, Hugo Grotius (b. 1583, d. 1645), who after the manner of his time played in the course of his career the diverse rôles of statesman, jurist, theologian, and man of letters. He was an Arminian, and he suffered grievous persecution at the hands of the dominant party in Calvinistic Holland.

His heresy, if indeed he was a heretic, was nothing else than the revolt of his gracious soul against the cruel orthodoxy of his day ; and this appears especially in his doctrine of the Atonement, which is expounded with characteristic erudition and charm in his too little known work *Defensio Fidei Catholicæ de Satisfactione Christi.* His argument is indeed directed against the doctrine of Socinus, the Arius of that period and the forerunner of modern Unitarianism ; but it is at the same time a tacit repudiation of the prevailing theory, which it essentially contravenes. It starts from the position that in the business of the Atonement God acts not as a judge or a creditor but as a ruler. A judge's office is the enforcement of the law, and a creditor exacts precise payment of his due ; but it is open to a ruler to show clemency or indulgence by relaxation or modification of the law. His concern is twofold—the welfare of his subjects and the maintenance of civil order. And these were the interests which God, the Ruler of the world, sought to conserve in the work of the Atonement. 'His disposition is to make man happy and blessed, but this He cannot do while that horrible and eternal punishment continues.' It might seem that a simple remedy lay in remitting the penalty of sin ; but this would have been fatal to both the interests involved. It would have violated the governmental order of the world, and thus, no less but even more than the infliction of punishment, it would have defeated His supreme end—the welfare of man, since it

would have emboldened man to persist in
sin. 'Every failure to punish sin carries this
consequence, that sins are less accounted ;
just as, on the contrary, the readiest reason
for refraining from sin is the dread of punishment.' Hence the simple remission of punishment would have been no remedy ; it would
rather have betrayed man in deeper consequence and thus aggravated his case. And
therefore God's wisdom devised a better way.
He freeely forgave man, but He did not let
sin go unpunished. Christ bore the punishment, that man might at once escape it and
by so signal an example be deterred from
farther sin. 'Hereby God not only attested
His hatred against all sins and forthwith by
this act deterred us from sins (for it is an
easy inference : If God would not remit sins
even to the penitent unless by Christ's undertaking the punishments, much less will He
suffer the contumacious to go unavenged),
but in a signal manner moreover disclosed His
supreme love and benevolence toward us,
because, that is to say, He to whom the
punishing of sins was not "a thing in-
different," spared us, but did it at such a

cost that, rather than let them go wholly
unpunished, He delivered up His Only-
begotten Son to punishments for those sins.
Plainly, as it was said by the ancients of
pardon that it is " neither according to law
nor against law but above law and for law," [1]
that would be most true of this divine grace.
It is " above law " because we are not
punished, it is " for law " because punishment
is not omitted ; and therefore is remission
made that for the future we may live unto
the Divine Law.'

Thus, briefly expressed, the theory of
Grotius is that the Atonement was not a
penal satisfaction for the sins of the past
but a penal example for the prevention of
sins in the future.

---

[1] οὐδὲ κατὰ νόμον οὐδὲ κατὰ νόμου ἀλλὰ ὑπὲρ νόμον καὶ
ὑπὲρ νόμου.

THE MODERN SPIRIT

THE MODERN SPIRIT

' Does a week pass without the announcement
of the discovery of a new comet in the sky, a
new star in the heaven, twinkling dimly out of
a yet farther distance, and only now becoming
visible to human ken though existent for ever
and ever ?   So let us hope divine truths may be
shining, and regions of light and love extant,
which Geneva glasses cannot yet perceive, and
are beyond the focus of Roman telescopes.'—
THACKERAY, *The Newcomes,* lxv.

WE have now reviewed the three types of A new age.
soteriological doctrine belonging to the three
large periods of Christian history — the
Patristic Period, the Mediæval, and the
Post-Reformation. Each was fashioned by
the spirit of its age and passed away when a
new age dawned and a new spirit emerged.
The Patristic Period was the age of brigandage
and warfare, and its doctrine of the Atonement
was the Ransom Theory ;   the Mediæval
Period was the age of Chivalry, and its
doctrine of the Atonement was the Satisfaction Theory ;   the Post-Reformation Period

was the age of Absolute Monarchy and Jurisprudence, and its doctrine of the Atonement was the Forensic Theory. And this theory has gone the way of its predecessors. So long as the intellectual order which created it continued, it was a living and satisfying doctrine. It interpreted the infinite truth in intelligible terms, and commended it to the mind of the age. But that age has now passed away, and a new age has arisen with other and larger thoughts; and the old formula is no longer valid.

The duty of faith.

It still indeed persists, but its vitality is gone: it is withered like an uprooted tree. What happened in previous periods of transition is once more being enacted before our eyes. Just as St. Bernard clung to the outworn Ransom Theory and refused to let it go, fancying that its abandonment involved a denial of the truth which it so imperfectly expressed, so now some, unconscious of the new order, are content with the old formula; while others, recognising its insufficiency, labour to rehabilitate and readjust it, thus putting the new wine into the old wine-skins. It is a vain attempt. The Forensic Theory belongs to a bygone age. It has passed like its predecessors into the limbo of theological antiquities; and the task of faith is not to galvanise the dead past but to welcome the new order and reinterpret the ancient truth and commend it to the modern mind.

The question is : What is the formative spirit of the modern world, the fresh and larger mould which must shape the Church's interpretation of her Lord's redemptive work ? And there is no manner of doubt what the modern spirit is. It is the Scientific Spirit. And this is an all-pervading spirit; its influence has transformed every department of thought. It is the spirit which, amid all seeming confusion, discovers the unity of a steadfast purpose working out its way from age to age and ever tending toward a nobler order.

The new intellectual norm the scientific spirit.

It is indeed too early yet to reckon up the gain which has accrued, as though the new forces had already spent themselves and were not rather only beginning their beneficent work ; nevertheless there are two directions in which the modern spirit has already contributed toward a deeper understanding of the

Two contributions toward a deeper interpretation of the Atonement:

Christian revelation and, especially, toward a larger interpretation of the atoning work of our Lord.

1. Historical criticism.

1. It has taught us a juster appreciation of the nature and use of the Holy Scriptures, the sacred records of revelation. And this precious gain has been procured by the science of Historical Criticism, which is nothing else than the literary application of the scientific method.

A new conception of the Holy Scriptures.

The difference which it has made is easily defined. The old view was that the Bible was a storehouse of divine truth, and its contents were homogeneous and equipollent. It was an indiscriminate quarry whence the theologian might gather material for the construction of his dogmatic system ; and his method was to adduce passages at random from the inspired pages, finding ' proof-texts ' equally and indifferently in the Law, the Prophets, the Gospels, and the Epistles. This method Historical Criticism has invalidated and discredited. It has taught us that the Bible is not a single book, one homogeneous work, but in St. Jerome's phrase—as the very name ' the Bible,' that is ' the Books,'

(1) Not a homogeneous storehouse of doctrines, but the literature of revelation.

implies—'a divine library' (*biblotheca divina*),[1] a collection of the rich and varied literature of revelation, the record of God's redemptive dealings with His people, covering the long course of their history and representing their continuous progress in His knowledge and their ever fuller experience of His grace. Revelation was a historical development, and the Holy Scriptures are its record ; and the science of Criticism has taught us to arrange the extensive and varied material in historical order, to correlate its successive stages, to view each in its proper perspective, and to recognise throughout a continuous growth, a process of evolution, from the first dim dawn to the full noonday, 'the light of the knowledge of the glory of God in the face of Jesus Christ.'[2]

(2) Revelation a historical development.

---

[1] Hieronym. *Catal. Script. Eccles.* under *Eusebius Cæsareæ Palæstinæ.* It was not until the thirteenth century that the neut. plur. βιβλία was mistaken for a fem. sing.—ἡ βιβλία.

[2] This principle is luminously presented by Lessing in his work, *The Education of the Human Race*, with its thesis that 'what education is to the individual revelation is to the race.' The idea had been anticipated by St. Augustine. Cf. *De Civit.Dei*, x. xiv : 'Sicut autem unius hominis, ita humani generis, quod ad Dei populum pertinet, recta eruditio per quosdam articulos temporum tanquam ætatum profecit accessibus, ut a temporalibus ad· æterna capienda et a visibilibus ad invisibilia surgeretur.'

The norm of doctrine the perfect and final revelation.

Hence emerges a simple yet momentous principle : *the norm of Christian doctrine is the perfect and final revelation*. And this revelation is our Lord Jesus Christ. No doctrine is Christian which lacks His guarantee, which is not found, explicitly or by necessary implication, in Him—in His teaching, His work, or His Person.

Two errors :

The recognition of this principle will deliver us from two errors which have wrought much mischief and confusion in the formulation of Christian theology. One is the fatal error of interpreting the fulfilment in terms of its dim foreshadowings. The source of Christian doctrine is the New Testament, and the value of the Old Testament is that it shows how the truth which is perfectly revealed in the New, was adumbrated and shone ever clearer and clearer from age to age, and how at length its full disclosure satisfied the long yearning of the human soul. And hence, if we would know the truth, we must look not at the foreshadowing but at the substance, not at the prophecy but at the fulfilment. We must interpret the symbol by the reality, and not the reality by the symbol. Thus, the Levitical

(1) Interpretation of the fulfilment in terms of its foreshadowings.

sacrifices were types of the Sacrifice of Christ,
but we must in nowise reduce the Sacrifice of
Christ to the level of the Levitical sacrifices
or express the Christian Atonement in terms
of the Jewish ritual.

Then there is the hardly less fatal error of
reducing the perfect and final revelation to
the dimensions of its theological formulations.
It is indeed true that Christianity is the com-
pletion of the long process of historic revelation. The Incarnate Word is God's full and
therefore His last word to the world. But
it does not follow that theological doctrines
are final. The revelation in Christ is infinite,
but a doctrine is merely a human definition,
and no human definition can ever compass the
infinite truth. 'The Faith which was once
for all delivered unto the saints' abides from
generation to generation, but there is ceaseless
progress in the Church's understanding of it,
and her definitions must be continually modi-
fied and her doctrine reformulated as she is
led by the Holy Spirit into a larger appreciation of her inexhaustible heritage. There is
a precise analogy here between theological
and physical science. 'There are,' says Sir

(2) Reduction
of the infinite
revelation to
the dimensions
of its dogmatic
formulations.

Jude 3, R.V.

I

Thomas Browne in his *Religio Medici*, ' two books from whence I collect my Divinity : beside the written one of God, another of his servant Nature, that universal and public manuscript that lies expans'd unto the eyes of all.'   The book of Nature is the study of physical science ; and its revelation is complete.   Yet patient investigation is ever discovering and appropriating more of its boundless wonder.   And so also the revelation in Christ is complete, but more of its treasures of wisdom and knowledge are continually coming to light, and the theological definitions which were accepted yesterday are no longer adequate, and to-day's definitions will be insufficient on the morrow.   The revelation abides ; but so long as the Church is taught by the Holy Spirit, her understanding of it must be ever deepening and broadening.

Theology a continual progress in understanding of the abiding revelation.

And thus a living theology is at once a ceaseless advance and a ceaseless return.   The new thought of each successive generation is always a clearer illumination of the ancient and enduring revelation in Christ ; and since the revelation is enshrined in the New Testament, theological progress is at the same time

The New Testament the norm.

a return to that sacred and imperishable record, especially to the holy Gospels. These are the heart of the New Testament, since 'in them,' says St. Irenæus,[1] 'Christ has His seat,' and He is evermore supreme. They present Him as He tabernacled among men in the days of His flesh, 'the Visible Image of the Invisible God.' The Epistles are indeed unspeakably precious. They are the testimonies of the men who had companied with Him, the eye-witnesses of His grace and truth ; yet they are subject to a twofold limitation. As we have seen, the Apostles testified only what they had experienced of the Lord's infinite grace, and it far transcended their experience. And they also interpreted Him in view of the passing needs and difficulties of their own generation. Their experiences and their interpretations are indeed permanently significant ; but the Lord was more than His Apostles, and His teaching, His work, and His person—what He said and, still more, what He did and, most of all, what He was—as these are presented by the Evangelists, constitute the supreme revelation. The

Especially the Gospels.

---

[1] III. xi. 11 : ἐν οἷς ἐγκαθίζεται Χριστός.

1 Cor. xiii. 9.

Col. i. 19, ii. 9.
Apostles 'knew in part and prophesied in part,' but 'in Him dwelleth all the fulness,' and 'He,' as Calvin affirms,[1] 'must be heard before them all in discoursing of His office.'

The test of a soteriological theory its conception of God.

See how this bears upon the problem before us. Since Salvation is the work of God, the sovereign determinant of the truth and value of a soteriological theory is the idea of God which it presupposes ; and here lies the fatal defect of all the theories which have hitherto prevailed in the Church : each has started from an idea of God which, whether true or false, is not the distinctive idea of the New Testament. Think of the Satisfaction Theory : what is its idea of God ? It defines Him as the Moral Governor of the world, whose 'honour' must be satisfied.[2] And what of the Forensic Theory ? It conceives God as the Judge who must vindicate 'justice.'[3] It may be indeed that these are

[1] *Instit.* II. xii. 4.

[2] *Cf.* Anselm, *Cur Deus Homo ?* I. xii : 'Ad nullum enim pertinet vindictam facere nisi ad illum qui Dominus est omnium ; nam cum terrenæ potestates hoc recte faciunt, ipse facit Deus a quo ad hoc ipsum sunt ordinatæ.'

[3] *Cf.* Turrett. *Instit. Theol.* XIV. x. ix : 'Deus quippe hîc non se habet tantum ut Creditor . . . et Dominus . . .

scriptural conceptions ; but neither is the
Scripture's final definition, neither is a distinctively Christian conception, and, most
important of all, neither is contained in the
teaching of our Lord. He never represented
God as the Moral Governor demanding
satisfaction for His violated honour, nor yet
as the Judge insisting on the vindication of
justice. He had one thought of God, and
only one. He proclaimed God as ' the
Heavenly Father,' and affirmed that all
men were His children and sinners His lost
children.

Our Lord's definition of God ' the Heavenly Father.'

This is the distinctively Christian conception of God, and no doctrine of the
Atonement is truly Christian which does not
start from this, and keep it steadfastly in
view. Whatever be the precise definition of
the Atonement, this much is certain—that
it is the dealing, not of a Ruler with rebels
or a Creditor with debtors or a Judge with
criminals, but of a Father with His erring
children. The Fatherhood of God is the

The Father-hood of God the foundation of the Atone-ment.

sed ut *Judex* et *Rector* Universi, ad quem solum pertinet
pœnæ inflictio vel a pœna liberatio, quia, ut agnoscunt
omnes Jurisconsulti, hoc tantum est supremi Magistratus
et τῆς ὑπερεχούσης ἐξουσίας.'

foundation of the Atonement, and on this we must build our doctrine.

2. Scientific elucidation of New Testament soteriology.

2. The modern spirit, which has created the science of Historical Criticism and thereby shown us the true perspective of the sacred literature of revelation, has also revolutionised our conceptions of the origin and constitution of the physical universe ; and hence has accrued a profounder and richer understanding of the Christian revelation. ' I venture to think that Darwin and the martyrs of natural science have done more to make the word of Christ intelligible than have Augustine and the theologians. It is little less than marvellous, the way in which the words of Jesus fit in with the forms of thought which are to-day current. They are life, generation, survival of the fit, perishing of the unfit, tree and fruit, multiplication by cell growth as yeast, operation by chemical contact as salt, dying of the lonely seed to produce much fruit, imposition of a higher form of life upon a lower by being born from above, grafting a new scion upon a wild stock, the phenomena of plant growth from the seed through the blade, the ear, and the matured grain, and,

finally, the attainment of an individual life which has an eternal quality.'[1]

And the light which has thus been poured on the entire domain of the Christian revelation, has not left the problem of the Atonement unillumined. The principle of the Solidarity of the Race with its corollary, the law of Heredity, has discovered a profound significance in the Pauline doctrine of Imputation, so long, as we shall see, a puzzle to theologians. It has taught us that humanity is no mere congeries of individuals but a vital organism, so inter-related in all its members that each lives in all. Vicarious Sacrifice is a universal law, and the Atonement is its supreme exemplification.

Imputation and the principles of solidarity and heredity.

Here then—in these twin conceptions, the Fatherhood of God and the organic unity of the human race—lies the mould which the modern spirit has furnished for a living doctrine of the Atonement, a rich and satisfying reinterpretation of the historic faith to the mind of our generation.

The modern mould of the doctrine of the Atonement.

[1] McConnell, *Evolution of Immortality*, pp. 135 f.

THE ATONEMENT IN THE LIGHT
OF THE MODERN SPIRIT

(1) FATHERHOOD AND SACRIFICE

' But if I knew Thy love even such,
    As tender and intense
As, tested by its human touch,
    Would satisfy my sense

' Of what a father never was
    But should be to his son,
My heart would leap for joy, because
    My rescue was begun.'

                GEORGE MACDONALD.

THE Fatherhood of God is a distinctively Christian conception. It occurs indeed in the Old Testament Scriptures, but never in the sense which it bore on the lips of our Lord. God was styled the Father of Israel, but the idea here is merely that He was the Creator, the maker and establisher of the nation. In this sense He was the Father of all the families of mankind ; and the distinction of the nation of Israel was that it was His 'firstborn,' holding the chief place in dignity and affection. And again, since the king was the head and representative of the

The Divine Fatherhood a distinctively Christian conception.

Cf. Dt. xxxii. 6 ; Is. xliii. 6, 7, lxiv. 8.

Cf. Ex. iv. 22.

nation, he was the son of God, and God was
his Father. ' I will establish the throne of
his kingdom for ever,' was the promise to
David. ' I will be his Father, and he shall
be My son.' ' He shall cry unto Me, Thou
art my Father, my God, and the Rock of
my salvation. I also will make him My
firstborn, the highest of the kings of the
earth.' His coronation was the king's birth,
and thus it is written in a coronation ode :
' I will tell of the decree : the Lord said unto
me, Thou art My son ; this day have I
begotten thee.'

It is true that there are not lacking in the
Old Testament suggestions of a more personal
and religious conception of the Divine Fatherhood. ' Like as a father pitieth his children,'
says the Psalmist, ' so the Lord pitieth them
that fear Him.' But this is a mere similitude ;
and the significant fact is that our Lord does
not merely liken God to a father, exhibiting
a fatherly tenderness ; He affirms that God
is our Father. And here is the distinctive
Christian truth. The Divine Fatherhood is
an actual kinship, and the evidence lies in the
transcendent fact of the Incarnation. What

2 Sam. vii. 13, 14.

Ps. lxxxix. 26, 27.

Ps. ii. 7.

Humanity's
divine kinship.

Ps. ciii. 13.

does it mean that it was possible for the Word to be made flesh and tabernacle among us, a man among men yet remaining God?[1] It means, it must mean, that there is an essential *Cf.* 2 Pet. i. 4. kinship, a community of nature, between God and man. 'Both He that sanctifieth Heb. ii. 11, 14. and they that are sanctified are all of one:[2] for which cause He is not ashamed to call them brethren. . . . Since then the children are sharers in flesh and blood, He also in like manner partook of the same.'

This truth has been profoundly elucidated 'The Image by St. Paul. On the first page of the Holy of God.' Scriptures it is written that 'God created Gen. i. 26, 27. man in His own image, after His own likeness'; and that primal image, the Archetype of humanity, the Apostle declares, was the Eternal Son of God. He is 'the image of the Col. i. 15. invisible God, the firstborn of all creation';

---

[1] *Cf.* Aug. *In Joan. Ev. Tract.* viii. 3: 'Neque enim sic factus est homo ut perderet quod Deus esset: accessit illi homo, non amissus est Deus.'

[2] ἐξ ἑνὸς πάντες. The ellipse is variously supplied as ἑνός is taken as masc. or neut. (1) θεοῦ (Fath., Alford); Adam (Erasm., Bez.); Abraham (Beng.). (2) σπέρματος or αἵματος (Carpz.); *ex communi massa* (Cappell.); *ex una natura* (Calv.). *Cf.* Acts xvii. 26: ἐποίησέν τε ἐξ ἑνὸς πᾶν ἔθνος ἀνθρώπων, where T.R. has ἐξ ἑνὸς αἵματος.

Rom. viii. 29.

and God ' foreordained us to be conformed to the image of His Son, that He might be the firstborn among many brethren.' And thus God is our Father in Christ, and the Incarnation is the revelation of our divine kinship and the realisation of the essential oneness of God and humanity. Sin has dimmed and defaced the divine image in our souls, and redemption is its restoration, ' our renewal after the image of Him that created us,' our ' transformation into the same image from glory to glory.' 'I confess, O Lord,' says St. Anselm,[1] 'and render thanks that Thou hast created in me this Thine image, that I may be mindful of Thee, may think of Thee, may love Thee. But so wasted is it by the attrition of vices, so darkened by the smoke of sins, that it cannot do what it was made to do, unless Thou renew and refashion it.'

Col. iii. 10.

2 Cor. iii. 18.

The Fatherhood of God is thus a vital truth of the Christian revelation ; and hence it is no wonder that it should figure so largely in our Lord's teaching. ' The Heavenly Father ' was His one name for God, and in

Our Lord's doctrine of the Divine Fatherhood.

[1] *Proslogion*, i.

the most beautiful and gracious of His parables—the Parable of the Prodigal Son —He has unfolded its significance, exhibiting two corollaries of the idea which constitute the foundation of Christian theology and especially of the doctrine of the Atonement.

One is the universality of the Divine Fatherhood. All the children of men are sons of God, and they are all dear to His heart. The prodigal in the parable stands for the sinner ; and it was not only after his return home in penitence that he was a son. He had been a son ere he left his father's house, and he remained a son all the while he was in the far country, rioting in excess and starving among the swine. What constitutes sonship is kinship, and kinship is indissoluble. A servant may quit his master's service and be his servant no longer ; but a son cannot unmake his sonship. He may quit his father's house and break his father's heart ; but he is his son still, and he can never be anything else. His father may disinherit him, but he cannot defiliate him. Milton expresses this truth with startling

Lk. xv. 11-32.

Two implicates :

1. The universality of the Fatherhood of God.

Sonship indissoluble.

audacity when he represents the rebel Satan as reasoning thus :[1]

> ' The Son of God I also am, or was ;
> And if I was, I am ; relation stands ;
> All men are sons of God.'

Once a son, always a son ; and neither depravity on the son's part nor resentment, however just, on the father's can cancel the relationship.

A lost son a son still.

Thus the Heavenly Fatherhood is as wide as humanity. The children of men are all children of God. A believer is a son of God, and so also is an unbeliever ; and the difference, the radical and momentous difference, between them is that the latter is a son *still lost*, while the former is a son who *has returned home*. The believer too was once in the far country, and he is a son who ' was lost and is found,' whereas the unbeliever is a son who is lost and not found as yet, but still remembered and desired ; and the Father's heart will never be satisfied until the wanderer is restored. And thus that term ' lost ' is one which, like many another

---

[1] *Paradise Regained*, iv. 518-20.

in the New Testament, has suffered grievous perversion in common parlance. When we speak of ' a lost soul,' we mean one doomed to final perdition ; but on the lips of our Lord the word has always a note of tenderness and a gleam of hope. Remember His gracious saying : ' The Son of Man came to seek and to save that which was lost.' There He defines the term. ' A lost soul ' is one who has gone astray, a wandered child whom the Father loves and yearns after, and has sent His Eternal Son, the Elder Brother, to seek and find and carry home. *Lk. xix. 10.*

This truth is movingly expressed in the parable by an exquisite touch which is unhappily obliterated in our English Version. When the returning prodigal began his confession, his father would not hear him out. He shouted to the servants : ' Bring forth the best robe '—so our translators have it— ' and put it on him.' But his words were literally ' Bring forth a robe—the first.' And what does this mean ? An illuminating commentary is furnished by that moving passage where our novelist describes old Dan'el Peggotty setting forth on his quest *Remembered and desired.*

K

for his little lost Em'ly :[1] 'The room was very neat and orderly. I saw in a moment that it was always kept prepared for her reception, and that he never went out but he thought it possible he might bring her home. . . . Without appearing to observe what he was doing, I saw how carefully he adjusted the little room, put a candle ready and the means of lighting it, arranged the bed, and finally took out of a drawer one of her dresses (I remember to have seen her wear it), neatly folded with some other garments, and a bonnet, which he placed upon a chair. He made no allusion to these clothes, neither did I. There they had been waiting for her, many and many a night, no doubt.' Here is the very picture which our Lord portrays in the parable. The prodigal had forgotten his father in the far country, but his father had never forgotten him. He had preserved his lost son's old robe and laid it by as a precious memorial. And now that the wanderer has returned, he would blot those unhappy days out of his remembrance. 'Bring forth a robe,' he cries ; not any robe, not the best in

[1] Dickens, *David Copperfield*, chap. xlvi.

the house, but 'the first,' his old robe, as
Matthew Henry puts it, ' the robe he wore
before he ran his ramble.' [1]   And the servants
would understand.   Many a time they had
seen their master take that old robe out and
unfold it tenderly with trembling hands and
survey it wistfully with dim eyes.   No other
robe would serve.   The past was forgiven,
and the father would banish it from his
remembrance as though it had never been.
The sweet old days had returned, and his
hungry heart was satisfied.

It may seem, however, as though this large
and gracious conception of our Blessed Lord
were narrowed down by the Pauline doctrine
of the Adoption of Believers.   For does not
adoption signify the reception of an alien
into one's home and his treatment as one's
child, though he can never be so in reality,
since it is kinship that makes sonship, and
kinship cannot be conferred ?   And thus,
unless we be sons of God originally, we can
never be His sons at all.   But what is St.
Paul's doctrine of Adoption ?   The Greek

Adoption and Fatherhood.

Cf. Rom. viii. 15, 23, ix. 4 ; Gal. iv. 5 ; Eph. i. 5.

---

[1] *Cf.* Aug. *Quœst. Ev.* ii. 33 : 'Stola prima est dignitas quam perdidit Adam.'

term (υἱοθεσία) denotes literally 'setting in the place of a son,' and it is remarkable that the Apostle employs it in accordance with this its proper signification. He expressly recognises the believer's antecedent sonship. In his thought God's adopted are not aliens introduced into God's family but disinherited sons reinstated in their birthright. 'God,' he says, 'sent forth His Son, born of a woman, born under the Law, that He might redeem them which were under the Law, that we might receive the adoption of sons,' or rather, 'that we might recover the status of sonship.' [1] Our sonship in Christ, the Apostle here affirms, is a recovered birthright; and, he proceeds, it is possible only because we are sons already : 'Because ye are sons, God sent forth the Spirit of His Son into our hearts, crying, Abba, Father.'

Gal. iv. 4-6.

And thus it appears that the Universal Fatherhood of God is a cardinal principle, a necessary postulate of Redemption ; and we

The imperishable Image of God.

---

[1] ἵνα τὴν υἱοθεσίαν ἀπολάβωμεν. ἀπολαμβάνειν is not simply 'receive' but 'get back what is rightfully one's own.' *Cf.* Chrys. : καλῶς εἶπεν "ἀπολάβωμεν," δεικνὺς ὀφειλομένην. Aug.: 'Nec dixit, accipiamus, sed *recipiamus* ; ut significaret hoc nos amisisse in Adam.'

return to that initial and fundamental truth, that we were ' created in the image of God,' and this archetypal image is the Eternal Son. It was imprinted upon us at the first, and, though broken and marred, it has never been obliterated ; though overlaid with a mass of corruption, it remains imperishable. For centuries a tradition prevailed among the citizens of Florence that somewhere in their midst lay a lost portrait by Giotto of their immortal poet Dante. It had disappeared amid the confusion of the sixteenth and seventeenth centuries ; and though it was sought after, it could never be found. The story went that it was in the Palace of the Podestà ; but the Palace had been converted into a gaol for common criminals, and there was no picture there. It seemed as though the treasure were lost beyond recovery ; but in the year 1840 a company of artists renewed the quest, and turned their attention to the chapel of the Palace—a chapel no longer, since it was employed as a storehouse, and its inner walls had been coated with plaster and whitewash. The explorers carefully removed the coarse encrustation, and at length they laid bare an exquisite fresco ; and there beneath the rubbish was the long-lost portrait.

Redemption its restoration.

And this is a parable. Every human soul, however defiled, bears the imperishable stamp of God's image ; and Redemption is the clearing away of the alien accretion and the discovery of the hidden glory. This is involved in the very word ' redemption,' and in all the other soteriological terms bearing the prefix *re*, which signifies ' again ' or ' anew '— *restoration, renewal, recreation, regeneration*. In every instance the idea is that the work of grace does not consist in making the sinner what he has never been but rather in making him what he was at the first in God's design, recalling a departed glory and reinstating him in a forfeited heritage. ' All men are sons of God,' ' created in His image, after His likeness.' The sacred impress may be dimmed and broken, but it is never obliterated or effaced ; and, whether at home or in the far country, all are sons of God.

2. The free-ness of the penitent's welcome.

This then is the first implicate of the Heavenly Fatherhood as our Lord presents it ; and the second is the freeness of the penitent's reception. The prodigal in the far country was still a son, and his father yearned for him. His door stood open ; and when the wanderer appeared, he received him with an overflowing welcome. He did not up-braid him ; he required neither apology nor reparation. This is the manner of an earthly father, and much more is it the manner of the Heavenly Father.

> ' Is 't enough I am sorry ?
> So children temporal fathers do appease ;
> Gods are more full of pity.' [1]

For human fatherhood is but a dim adumbration of the Divine Fatherhood, and the substance is more than the shadow. ' If ye, being evil, know how to give good gifts unto your children, how much more shall your Father which is in Heaven give good things to them that ask Him ? '

Mt. vii. 11.

Such is our Lord's representation of God's attitude toward penitent sinners ; and the significant fact is that He says nothing of ' propitiation ' according to the forensic interpretation of that term, nothing of ' the placation of God,' ' the appeasement of His anger,' or ' the satisfaction of His justice.'

No ' propitiation' in our Lord's doctrine.

[1] Shakespeare, *Cymbeline*, v. iv. 10-12.

Dogmatic
evasions:

The omission is conspicuous, and theologians, dominated by dogmatic prepossessions, have found it not a little disconcerting and have laboured to remedy it.

(1) 'The fatted calf' a propitiatory sacrifice.

St. Ambrose and others of the Fathers recognised in 'the fatted calf' a parabolic image of the Divine Victim and His Atoning Sacrifice.[1] If it were needful to criticise so fantastic a notion, it would suffice to observe that the supposed propitiation follows the reconciliation instead of preceding and procuring it.

(2) A parabolic representation incomplete.

In modern days it has frequently been argued that a parable exhibits only a single aspect of the truth, and since our Lord is here concerned particularly with God's welcome of the returning penitent, it is no surprise that He should have ignored the propitiation which has made the welcome possible. Nor indeed, it is alleged, is this the sole omission; for He says nothing in the parable of the father going

[1] Cf. Ambr. Expos. Evang. sec. Luc. vii. 232: 'Occiditur et vitulus saginatus, ut carnem Domini spirituali opimam virtute per gratiam sacramenti mysteriorum consortio restitutus epuletur. . . . Bene autem carnem vituli, quia sacerdotalis est victima, quæ pro peccatis fiebat.' Aug. Quæst. Ev. ii. 33 : 'Vitulus saginatus, ipse idem Dominus.' Euth. Zig. : μόσχος σιτευτός, τὸ ἅγιον σῶμα τοῦ Χριστοῦ.

in quest of the prodigal, though it is the very
heart of the Gospel that ' Christ Jesus came 1 Tim. i. 15.
into the world to save sinners.' The argu-
ment, however, is futile. The parable of the
Prodigal Son does not stand alone. It is the
last of a triad defining God's attitude toward
sinners ; and in each of its companions—
the parables of the Lost Sheep and the Lost Lk. xv. 3-10.
Piece of Silver—His quest for the lost is so
plainly portrayed that there was no need of
further elaboration. And, moreover, while
it is indeed a reasonable contention that a
parable expresses only a particular lesson
and takes no account of much else which is
nevertheless true and important, the question
here is whether the idea of ' the appeasement
of God's anger ' can be accounted a legitimate
and necessary supplement to the parable.
And the fact is that it were rather an open Propitiation an
impossible
supplement.
contradiction of our Lord's argument. For
it is the very foundation of the parable that
there was no anger in the father's heart against
his erring son but only an overflowing
tenderness. He needed no appeasement. It
was enough that his son had returned in
penitence ; and he took him to his breast

and would not listen to his premeditated confession.

This is our Lord's representation of God's attitude toward sinners, and it is plainly incompatible with the idea of a wrathful God who must be ' propitiated ' and demands that His justice be satisfied ere He forgives. Indeed that idea is not merely alien from our Lord's teaching but subversive of the fundamental truth of the Gospel ; for where there is satisfaction, there is no real forgiveness. This is an inevitable issue of the Forensic Theory, and if evidence be required, it is furnished by Francis Turrettin. If sin, he argues,[1] were merely a debt, then its payment by another would suffice for the liberation of the debtor. It would make no difference whether he paid the debt himself or another paid it on his behalf ; for in a pecuniary debt the consideration is not *who pays* but *what is paid,* and in accepting a vicarious payment of his due the creditor shows no indulgence or remission to the debtor. But sin is more than a debt. It is a crime ; and here the consideration is not only *what is paid* but also

[1] *Instit. Theol.* XIV. x. 8.

who pays. The punishment must be borne
by the sinner ; for, as the law demands
proper and personal obedience, it exacts also
proper and personal punishment. Hence,
were God merely the Judge, He must have
exacted of sinners the punishment of their
sin, since a judge's office is the enforcement
of the law ; but since He is also the Ruler, it
was open to Him, not indeed to cancel the law
and remit the punishment, but to relax the law
so far as to accept a substitute and inflict a
vicarious punishment. ' In the endurance of
the punishment, which was borne by Christ,
there is satisfaction, but in the admission and
acceptance of a Substitute there is remission.'
And this is all the forgiveness, this is the
farthest reach of grace, which the Forensic
Theory recognises.

Such is the issue of the forensic doctrine of
propitiation. The harm lies, however, not
in the term ' propitiation ' but in its forensic
interpretation. For the apostolic idea of
propitiation is not only far different from the
doctrine of the Protestant Scholastics but
absolutely accordant with the teaching of our
Lord. The term is infrequent in the apostolic

The apostolic idea of ' propitiation.'

Heb. ii. 17,
R.V.; 1 Jo. ii.
2, iv. 10; Rom.
ii. 25.

writings, occurring but four times—once in the Epistle to the Hebrews, twice in the first Epistle of St. John, and once, at all events according to the common interpretation, in St. Paul's Epistle to the Romans. There are here three cognate terms : the verb ἱλάσκεσθαι, ' propitiate ' or ' make propitiation,' and its derivatives, the noun ἱλασμός, ' propitiation,' and ἱλαστήριον, variously taken as a noun, ' propitiation,' and as an adjective, ' propitiatory.' And the question is what precisely these terms signify.

(1) ἱλάσκεσθαι.

Of the signification of the verb ἱλάσκεσθαι in classical Greek literature there is no dubiety. It meant to ' propitiate ' or ' appease,' especially to ' appease ' the anger of a god by a sacrificial offering.' [1] But this was a pagan notion, and in the Septuagint Version of the Old Testament the usage of the verb is widely different. The pagan term was redeemed by its enlistment in the service of revelation, and it is employed to render two Hebrew words— *kipper* (כִּפֶּר), ' make atonement,' and, in seven instances, *ṣalaḥ* (סָלַח), ' pardon,' ' forgive.'

A pagan term employed by the Septuagint.

---

[1] *Cf.* Hom. *Il.* i. 385: κελόμην θεὸν ἱλάσκεσθαι. 444: Φοίβῳ θ᾽ ἱερὴν ἑκατόμβην | ῥέξαι ὑπὲρ Δαναῶν ὄφρ᾽ ἱλασόμεσθα ἄνακτα. Plat. *Phæd.* 95 A.

The former of these Hebrew terms is, theo-The Hebrew original.
logically, the more important. In common
usage it signified ' cover,' and hence its soteriological sense is usually derived, to ' cover sin '
being to make atonement for it. But it
would rather seem that ' cover ' is a derivative
sense, and the root-idea of the verb is ' wipe '
or ' smear,' the meaning which it bears in
Syriac,[1] and which occurs also in Hebrew, as,
for instance, in the command to Noah that Gen. vi. 14.
he should ' smear (כָּפַרְתָּ) the ark with pitch.'
Hence naturally arise the various uses of the
verb in the Hebrew Scriptures. Thus, when a
covenant was ' disannulled,' it was said to be
' smeared over ' or ' wiped away ' ;[2] and so
also sin was ' smeared over ' or ' wiped away '
when it was forgiven.[3] And so it appears that
kipper is simply a picturesque synonym for
ṣalaḥ, ' forgive ' or ' be merciful.'

When the Septuagint translators addressed Investment of the Greek term with the Hebrew idea.
themselves to the task of rendering the
Hebrew Scriptures into Greek, they found

---

[1] *Cf.* Robertson Smith, *O. T. in Jew. Ch.*, p. 438, *n.* 5.

[2] *Cf.* Is. xxviii. 18 : וְכֻפַּר בְּרִיתְכֶם.

[3] *Cf.* Ps. lxv. 3 : פְּשָׁעֵינוּ אַתָּה תְכַפְּרֵם, ' as for our transgressions, Thou shalt purge them away.' LXX, ἱλάσῃ τὰς
ἀσεβείας.

themselves confronted by a peculiar and indeed insurmountable difficulty. It was one result of the providential discipline of the chosen people that soteriological ideas occupied a large place in their thought, and their language was singularly rich in soteriological terms. Those ideas, however, were unknown to the pagan world, and the Greek language lacked terms for their expression, and such terms as it possessed had a pagan colour. ἱλάσκεσθαι was its closest approximation to the Hebrew idea of 'forgiveness,' but it was a sorry substitute. It carried the notion of the appeasement of an angry god, and that was a pagan notion which revelation had eradicated from the Hebrew religion. Nevertheless the term was the best available, and the translators were constrained to employ it. But they employed it definitively, sedulously eliminating its pagan implicate; and this appears most impressively from the circumstance that, whereas in classical literature ἱλάσκεσθαι, as we have seen, takes an accusative of the deity propitiated as its direct object, it is never so construed in the Septuagint. Its object there is not *God* but *sin*.[1] And thus, since 'propitiate sin' is an impossible idea, it appears that in their use of the verb the Septuagint translators have deliberately altered its signification, stripping it of its proper sense of 'propitiate,' and investing it with the sense of its conventional Hebrew equivalent, *kipper*, 'wipe out' or 'purge away.'[2]

Such is the *usus loquendi* of the Greek Version of the Old Testament, and it is followed in the apostolic writings. Here the verb ἱλάσκεσθαι occurs only once : 'It behoved Him in all things to be made like unto His brethren, that He might be a merciful and faithful High Priest in things pertaining to God, to make propitiation for the sins of the people' (εἰς τὸ ἱλάσκεσθαι τὰς ἁμαρτίας τοῦ λαοῦ), that is, according to the scriptural idea, 'to make atonement for' or

So in apostolic writings.

Heb. ii. 17.

---

[1] Except in a single instance—Zech. vii. 2 : ἐξιλάσασθαι τὸν Κύριον. Here, however, the Hebrew is לְחַלּוֹת אֶת־פְּנֵי יְהוָה, rightly rendered in R.V. 'to entreat the favour of the Lord,' literally 'to smooth the face of the Lord.'

[2] It is significant that in Prov. xvi. 14 : 'The wrath of a king is as messengers of death : but a wise man will pacify it (יְכַפְּרֶנָּה),' the LXX Version mistranslates ἐξιλάσεται αὐτόν, 'will propitiate him.' There was no scruple about the propitiation of an angry king.

'purge away the sins of the people.' The object of the 'propitiation' is not God but the sins.

(2) ἱλασμός. Then there is St. John's designation of our Lord as 'a propitiation for our sins' (ἱλασμὸς περὶ τῶν ἁμαρτιῶν ἡμῶν). ἱλασμός is the Septuagint's rendering of the Hebrew *kip-purim* ; and *kippurim* is the cognate noun of the verb *kipper*, and in our English Versions, just as the verb is rendered 'atone,' so the noun is rendered 'atonement.' Thus 'the Lev. xxiii. 27, xxv. 9. Day of Atonement' is in Hebrew *yom hak-kippurim* (יוֹם הַכִּפֻּרִים) and in the Septuagint ἡ ἡμέρα τοῦ ἱλασμοῦ (ἐξιλασμοῦ). And the noun ἱλασμός has experienced in its use by the Septuagint the same transfiguration which we have observed in the verb ἱλάσκεσθαι. The pagan idea of 'propitiation' has been elimi- Cf. Ex. xxix. 36, xxx. 10. nated, and this appears from two facts. One is that elsewhere in the Septuagint *kippurim* is rendered 'purgation' (καθαρισμός) ; and the Ps. cxxx. 4. other is that in at least one instance ἱλασμός stands for *ṣeliḥah* (סְלִיחָה), 'forgiveness.'

(3) ἱλαστήριον. The sole remaining instance of the apos-
Rom. iii. 25. tolic use of this vexed term is the Pauline ἱλασ-τήριον, and it is peculiarly significant. It has

generally been interpreted sacrificially; but here the exegetical agreement ceases, and it has been debated whether it be, as both our Versions take it, a noun—'whom God hath set forth to be a propitiation,' or, as the Revisers indicate in their marginal note, an adjective—'whom God hath set forth to be propitiatory.' This uncertainty provokes inquiry, and a truer interpretation is presented by consideration of the scriptural usage of the term. It occurs once and only once again in the New Testament—in that passage in the Epistle to the Hebrews where the furniture _{Heb. ix. 5.} of the Holy of Holies is detailed: the Ark of the Covenant with its sacred contents, and 'above it cherubim of glory overshadowing the ἱλαστήριον.' Here the signification of the term stands in no manner of doubt. It means 'the Mercy-seat'; and this is the 'The Mercy-seat.' meaning which it always bears in the Old Testament. It is the Septuagint's rendering of the Hebrew *kapporeth* (כַּפֹּרֶת), the 'covering' or lid of the Ark of the Covenant, which _{Ex. xxv. 17-22.} carried at either end a golden cherub with overshadowing wings. This is the constant signification of the term alike in the Greek

L

Version of the Old Testament Scriptures and in Hellenistic literature ;[1] and so Origen understood it in this Pauline passage.[2] Indeed it can mean nothing else, and its association with the alien idea of ' propitiation ' is at once an exegetical blunder and a theological misfortune. It is a nobler thought that the Apostle here expresses. He styles our Lord Jesus Christ ' the Mercy-seat,' the true meeting-place between God and sinners. It is indeed a bold metaphor, but it is none too bold. Does not St. John likewise style the Incarnate Word ' the Shekinah,' the cloud of glory which overshadowed the Mercy-seat, the visible token of God's presence ?[3] And St. Ignatius calls God the ' one Sanctuary ' and Christ the ' one Altar.'[4] Observe how the metaphor accords with the argument of

[1] Cf. Philo, De Profugis, p. 561 (Mangey) : τῆς δ' ἵλεω δυνάμεως, τὸ ἐπίθεμα τῆς κιβωτοῦ· καλεῖ δ'αὐτὸ ' ἱλαστήριον '. . . . λέγεται γάρ· ' λαλήσω σοι ἄνωθεν τοῦ ἱλαστηρίου ἀνὰ μέσον τῶν δυοῖν Χερουβίμ ' (Ex. xxv. 22).

[2] In Epist. ad Rom. Comment. iii. 8.

[3] Jo. i. 14 : καὶ ὁ Λόγος σὰρξ ἐγένετο καὶ ἐσκήνωσεν ἐν ἡμῖν, καὶ ἐθεασάμεθα τὴν δόξαν αὐτοῦ. By reason of the assonance σκηνή (σκηνόω) was employed to represent the Targumist שְׁכִינָה (Shekinah). Cf. Rev. vii. 15, xxi. 3; 2 Cor. xii. 9.

[4] Magnes. vii. Cf. Heb. xiii. 10.

the passage. The ancient Mercy-seat was secluded in the Holy of Holies, and was visited *Cf.* Heb. ix. 25. by the High Priest alone once every year ; but our Mercy-seat ' God hath set forth,' ever open to the approach of every penitent. And again, as the High Priest sprinkled the blood *Cf.* Lev. xvi. 14, 15. of the sacrifice upon the Mercy-seat in the Holy of Holies, so ' God hath set forth Christ ἱλαστήριον διὰ πίστεως ἐν τῷ αὐτοῦ αἵματι, a Mercy-seat through faith, besprinkled with His blood.'

These are the only instances where ἱλάσ- Our Lord's use of ἱλάσθητι. κεσθαι and its derivatives occur in the apostolic writings, and it appears how studiously the pagan idea of ' propitiation ' in the sense of appeasing an angry God is excluded. The ' propitiation ' is never wrought by the penitent upon God ; it is wrought by God upon the penitent's sin. It signifies not the sinner's placation of God, the appeasement of His anger, the satisfaction of His justice, but God's forgiveness and purgation of the sinner's guilt. There is, however, one other instance Lk. xviii. 13. of the word in the New Testament, and this is the prayer of the publican in our Lord's parable : ὁ Θεός, ἱλάσθητί μοι τῷ ἁμαρτωλῷ,

'God, be merciful to me, the sinner.' It seems at the first glance as though there were here a plain departure from the scriptural usage and a reversion to the pagan notion. For ἱλάσθητι is a passive imperative, and it means literally, as the Revisers observe in their marginal note, 'be propitiated.' But the exception is only apparent. ἱλάσθητι, with its more frequent variant ἵλεως ἔσῃ, is a liturgical formula in the Septuagint. It occurs, for example, in Daniel's prayer :

Dan. ix. 19.

'O Lord, hear ; O Lord, forgive' (ἱλάσθητι, Κύριε), and again in King Solomon's prayer :

1 Ki. viii. 34, 36, 39.

'Hear Thou in Heaven, and forgive the sin of Thy people Israel' (καὶ ἵλεως ἔσῃ ταῖς ἁμαρτίαις τοῦ λαοῦ σου Ἰσραήλ). And the significant fact is that in every such instance the Hebrew verb is ṣalaḥ, and ṣalaḥ means simply 'pardon,' 'forgive,' 'be merciful.'[1] Thus the idea of 'propitiation' has no place in the publican's prayer, and 'God, be merciful to me' is its true rendering.

The exegetical issue is clear, and it is thus

---

[1] *Cf.* 2 Ki. v. 18 : יִסְלַח־נָא יְהוָה לְעַבְדֶּךָ, ἱλάσεται Κύριος τῷ δούλῳ σου, 'the Lord pardon thy servant.' Ps. xxv. 11 : וְסָלַחְתָּ לַעֲוֹנִי, ἱλάσῃ τῇ ἁμαρτίᾳ μου, 'pardon mine iniquity.'

stated by the late Bishop Westcott :[1] 'The scriptural conception of ἱλάσκεσθαι is not that of appeasing one who is angry, with a personal feeling, against the offender ; but of altering the character of that which from without occasions a necessary alienation, and interposes an inevitable obstacle to fellowship. Such phrases as "propitiating God" and God "being reconciled" are foreign to the language of the New Testament.   Man is reconciled to God (2 Cor. v. 18 ff. ; Rom. v. 10 f.).   There is a "propitiation" in the matter of the sin or of the sinner.   The love of God is the same throughout ; but He "cannot" in virtue of His very Nature welcome the impenitent and sinful : and more than this, He "cannot" treat sin as if it were not sin.'   The term 'propitiation' never occurs in the English Version of the Old Testament Scriptures ; and the reason is that the Version was made from the Hebrew text, and the idea of 'propitiation' is alien from the Hebrew thought and language.   It is a pagan idea, and it was introduced into the Greek Version by an unfortunate necessity ; but the Greek trans-

Exegetical issue : the scriptural idea not 'propitia-tion' but 'atonement.'

---

[1] *The Epistles of St. John*, p. 87.

lators, while employing the term which signified 'propitiation,' were careful to divest it
of its pagan signification and invest it with
the Hebrew idea. Their Greek term passed
into the New Testament vocabulary ; and
there it is defined, with no less clearness, in
the sense which the scriptural revelation
demands. Hence, if we would translate the
New Testament truly, reproducing not its
language but its thought, then we must
banish the term ' propitiation ' from its pages,
and substitute the Old Testament's term
'atonement.' 'It behoved Him in all things
to be made like unto His brethren, that
He might be a merciful and faithful High
Priest in things pertaining to God, *to make
atonement for the sins of the people.*' ' He is
an atonement for our sins ; and not for ours
only, but also for the whole world.' ' Herein
is love, not that we loved God, but that He
loved us, and sent His Son, *an atonement for
our sins.*'

'Atonement'
in our Lord's
teaching.

It is thus no marvel that there is nothing
in the parable of the Prodigal Son of ' propitiation,' nothing of ' placation of God,'
' appeasement of His anger,' or ' satisfaction

of His justice.' But is there nothing of 'atonement,' nothing of 'sacrifice'? In truth this is the very heart of the parable. The immortal story is nothing else than our Lord's doctrine of Redemption; and if we consider it, we shall understand what the Atonement really means.

Did the sin of the prodigal cost his father nothing? Nay, it was the father who suffered most; indeed he was the only sufferer so long as his son was in the far country, 'wasting his substance with riotous living,' and his gladness when the wanderer returned is the measure of the anguish which had torn his heart. It was vicarious suffering: the prodigal sinned, but it was his father who 'bore the grief and carried the sorrow.' And this is the Sacrifice of the Atonement. It is the anguish which His children's sin costs the Heavenly Father, and the travail which He has endured to bring them home. Observe, it is His Fatherhood which makes the Sacrifice inevitable. Were He merely the Moral Governor, He would resent our sin as a violation of the moral order; were He merely the Judge, He would condemn it as a crime and

Vicarious sacrifice in the Parable of the Prodigal Son.

A necessity of Fatherhood.

exact the legal penalty ; but because He is
our Father, it pierces His heart. The sin
is ours, but because He loves us, the sorrow is
His. For love is in its very essence a vicarious principle.

> ' Love seeketh not itself to please,
>   Nor for itself hath any care,
>   But for another gives its ease,
>   And builds a heaven in hell's despair.'

Since God is our Father, our sin is His sorrow.
Its burden lies on Him. He is ' wounded for
our transgressions, and bruised for our
iniquities.'

Christ one with
the Father.

Jo. x. 30.

Jo. xiv. 9.

And this is the meaning of the Cross. Remember that basal truth of the Christian
revelation—that Christ and the Father are
one, so truly one in character, purpose, and
disposition toward sinners that He could say :
' He that hath seen Me hath seen the Father.'
Whatever Christ was, the Father was also ;
whatever He did, the Father did in Him.
And when we see Him bearing the load of the
world's guilt and ' giving His life a ransom
for many,' what is it that we see ? It is not
a merciful Saviour appeasing an angry God ;
for if Christ and God be one, then nothing

is true of either which is not true of the other, and it might as reasonably be affirmed that God appeased Christ as that Christ appeased God. The Sacrifice for the sin of the world was God's Sacrifice. It was not the world's sacrifice to God but God's sacrifice for the world. It was not offered *to* Him ; it was offered *by* Him ; [1] and the spectacle which it displays is the Eternal Father through His Eternal Son identifying Himself, in vicarious love, with His erring children of men and taking upon Himself the burden of their sin and sorrow.

His Sacrifice God's Sacrifice.

It is told that, when ' the good Earl of Derby ' was on his deathbed, his house-keeper, a pious Methodist, was reading to him that fine old Methodist hymn, 'All ye that pass by'; and when she had read the lines :

A satisfaction not of justice but of love.

> ' The Lord in the day of His anger did lay
> Our sins on the Lamb, and He bore them away,'

---

[1] Since sacrifice means voluntary endurance of loss and suffering for a dear and sacred cause, the question *to whom* it is offered never arises. The relevant questions are *by whom* and *for whom*. Her sacrifice of blood and treasure in war is offered *by* a brave nation *for* freedom. The question *to whom* relates not to a sacrifice but to an indemnity.

he interrupted her. 'Stop! Don't you think, Mrs. Brass, that ought to be "The Lord in the day of His *mercy* did lay"?' That hits the mark. The Atonement is more, far more and far better, than a sacrifice to satisfy God's *justice*; it is a sacrifice to satisfy His *love*. Christ died for love of sinners; 'and God was in Christ reconciling the world unto Himself.' 'Christ suffered for sins once, the Righteous for the unrighteous,' not 'that He might bring God to us,' but 'that He might bring us to God.' For He was the Eternal Son of God Incarnate, and in His Passion the heart of the Eternal Father was revealed.

1 Pet. iii. 18.

(2) THE SATISFACTION OF MAN'S MORAL INSTINCTS

' Canst thou not minister to a mind diseased,
Pluck from the memory a rooted sorrow,
Raze out the written troubles of the brain,
And with some sweet oblivious antidote
Cleanse the stuff'd bosom of that perilous stuff
Which weighs upon the heart ? '

SHAKESPEARE.

WE have now considered two truths which are fundamental in the construction of a scriptural doctrine of the Atonement. The first is that central fact of the Christian revelation, that God is more than the Creator and Governor of the world or the King and Judge of men ; He is the Heavenly Father, and He has a Father's tenderness and compassion for the children of men. And sinners are still His children—His lost children, and therefore peculiarly dear to Him, the objects of His special solicitude and desire. And the second is that our Lord Jesus Christ was ' the Visible Image of the Invisible God,' the manifestation

Two fundamental truths : (1) God's Universal Fatherhood.

(2) Christ's oneness with God.

of the Unseen Father. He and the Father were one, and all that He was and did the Father was and did through Him. His heart was the Father's heart. His thoughts the Father's thoughts, His purposes the Father's purposes, and His Sacrifice the Father's Sacrifice.

> ' So, to our mortal eyes subdued,
>   Flesh-veiled, but not concealed,
> We know in thee the fatherhood
>   And heart of God revealed.
>
> ' The homage that we render thee
>   Is still our Father's own ;
> No jealous claim or rivalry
>   Divides the Cross and Throne.'

The Atonement is God's Sacrifice for the sin of the world ; it is the sorrow which His children's misdoing cost the Father, the travail which He bore in bringing His wanderers home. The whole truth lies in that declaration of the 2 Cor. v. 18-21, Apostle : ' All things are of God, who reconciled us to Himself through Christ, and gave unto us the ministry of reconciliation ; to wit, that God was in Christ reconciling the world unto Himself, not reckoning unto them their trespasses, and having committed unto us the word of reconciliation. We are ambassadors therefore on behalf of Christ, as though God were intreating you by us : we beseech you on behalf of Christ, be ye reconciled to God. Him who knew no sin He made to be sin on our behalf ; that we might become the righteousness of God in Him.'

Here a fresh problem arises. When the Apostle says that in order that we might become the righteousness of God in Him, God made Him who knew no sin to be sin on our behalf, he represents the Vicarious Passion of our Lord as a soteriological necessity. This is the constant doctrine of the New Testament Scriptures, and our Lord affirmed it with peculiar emphasis. 'The Son of Man,' He said ere it came to pass, 'must suffer many things, and be rejected by the Elders, and the Chief Priests, and the Scribes, and be killed, and after three days rise again.' And afterwards : 'Behoved it not the Christ to suffer these things, and to enter into His glory ?' And the question is wherein that necessity lay; why He had to suffer and die in order that sinners might be reconciled to God.

It is no small merit of the historic theories of

A fresh problem : The necessity of an atoning sacrifice.

Mk. viii. 31.

Lk. xxiv. 26.

Obvious on
the historic
theories.

the Atonement and, perhaps, not the least reason of the influence which they exerted while they retained their vitality, that each presented a clear and intelligible answer to this question. On the Patristic Theory the Death of Christ was the ransom which delivered sinners from the tyranny of Satan; on the Mediæval Theory it was a satisfaction to God's honour; and on the Post-Reformation Theory it was a satisfaction to His justice. The first theory and the second are now mere 'fossil remains,' possessing only an historical interest. And as for the third, it too has passed into the limbo of dogmatic antiquities; but it still lingers in the Church like a feeble ghost, a tradition of a departed age; nor will it vanish until the abiding question has been answered afresh and the Atoning Sacrifice is set securely in the new intellectual order.

Apparently
eliminated
by the
Fatherhood
of God.

It may seem as though all necessity for a sacrifice were eliminated by the recognition of God's Universal Fatherhood and the definition of the Atonement as the world's reconciliation to Him and not His reconciliation to the world. In ancient Athens after a civil war it was

customary that an ' amnesty ' should be proclaimed, an act of oblivion, decreeing that the
past should be forgotten, no inquiry insti-
tuted, no penalty imposed. ' Let bygones be
bygones ' was the healing policy. And would
it not have sufficed that, in addressing Himself to the task of reconciling the world unto
Himself, God should, without more ado,
' proclaim an amnesty,' offering a free pardon
to every returning penitent ?

Untenable as his theory may be, there is
still reason in St. Anselm's argument that in
forgiving sin it was necessary for God as the
Moral Governor of the world to vindicate
the moral order ; and Grotius penetrated yet
nearer to the heart of the problem when he
insisted that the interest involved was less
God's honour than our welfare. This, in a
profounder sense than Grotius perceived, is
the essential truth. Man's need was God's
primary concern in the Atonement, and it
could not be met without a Sacrifice. A
Gospel which merely proclaimed an amnesty
would be unavailing for the satisfaction of
the soul's requirements. It would bring no
peace ; for such is the constitution of our

Man's need
God's chief
concern.

No peace
without
expiation.

moral nature that there is no peace for a sinner unless his sin be expiated. This is no mere theological fiction but a principle which has been recognised by moralists in all ages. Thus in Plato's *Gorgias* [1] Socrates maintains and demonstrates a double thesis : that it is a worse evil to do wrong than to suffer wrong, and that it is better for the wrongdoer to be punished than to go unpunished. He may succeed in his wrongdoing, and perhaps be envied and admired by the world ; nevertheless he is miserable, nor can he ever be otherwise until he confesses the wrong and abides its consequences. In his tragedy of the *Eumenides* Æschylus, that stern preacher of righteousness, had already proclaimed the same grim truth, depicting, in the awful imagery of the ancient mythology, how the moment a crime had been committed the Furies, which were nothing else than the terrors of Conscience, went on the criminal's track and pursued him remorselessly, until blood had atoned for blood. And Coleridge [2] has related an impressive story of a young Italian artist who, in resentment of an insult,

[1] 475 f.   [2] *Table Talk*, May 1, 1823.

assassinated his patron at Rome and fled from justice. He escaped to Germany and, settling at Hamburg, devoted himself there to his profession. He prospered, and he was secure from detection and retribution ; yet he had no peace. The Furies were on his track. The memory of his crime haunted him day and night, and he had never a moment's respite. Wherever he might be, he seemed to hear his victim's voice calling his name and see his face staring at him. At length he could endure it no longer, and he resolved to return to Rome and surrender himself to justice and expiate his guilt on the scaffold.

Nor is this dire law limited to grave crimes. It operates equally in lesser delinquencies ; and a curious instance was furnished recently by a newspaper report of the proceedings at a meeting of a Scottish Town Council, where the Provost submitted a letter which he had received from Washington, U.S.A. It bore the writer's signature, and it ran thus : ' I have to confess that I did steal an apple from a stand of some description in the Cowgate as far back as about forty years ago, and I send you a dollar as payment to be used in

M

whatever way you think best, and I want you to forgive me for it.' His guilt had clung to the sinner ; it had followed him to the other side of the world, and haunted him all those long years ; and he could not rest until he had faced it and endured its consequences. Repentance was not enough. His sin had to be adequately dealt with. It demanded expiation ; and expiation means open confession and full reparation.

Legal expiation personal. In this stern and inexorable law lies the necessity of an atoning sacrifice for the sin of the world. It is primarily a human necessity. It is indeed a divine necessity also ; not because God's justice demands satisfaction or because His wrath must be appeased, but because Love is vicarious and the sin of His children lays a burden of sorrow on the Father's heart. Primarily, however, it is a human necessity. It is demanded by man's moral instincts. Expiation is the sinner's only way of peace ; and ' we have peace with God through our Lord Jesus Christ ' inasmuch as He ' suffered for sins once, the Righteous for the unrighteous.' Here, however, a question arises : Is not expiation necessarily personal ? Conscience, the soul's moral instinct, demands not merely that the penalty be endured but that it be endured by the offender. It will not satisfy him that a third party has borne it for him. That would indeed suffice to absolve him from the vengeance of the person he has wronged ; but it would merely shift the debt and aggravate his remorse. If his moral nature were sound, he could never rest until he had dealt with the benefactor who had interposed on his behalf. And our Lord's Sacrifice was not personal. It was vicarious. He ' suffered for sins, the Righteous for the unrighteous ' ; and this, on legal terms, is not an expiation ; it is merely a transference of the obligation. And there is no peace for the sinner until he has confessed his sin and endured the penalty.

On the Forensic Theory of the Atonement The vicarious this difficulty is insuperable. So long as God expiation of Love. is conceived as the Judge, there is no efficacy in a vicarious sacrifice. The substitution of a sinless victim might indeed satisfy the divine justice and appease the divine wrath ; but, as we have seen, it would involve a flagrant illegality, and it would not satisfy the sinner's moral instincts or bring peace to his conscience. View God, however, as our Lord has taught us, not as the Judge but as the Father; and then the reasonableness of a vicarious expiation appears. There is one way, and only one way, of peace without reparation; and this is by the intervention of Love—the lifting of the affair out of the domain of strict legality, and the discovery by the sinner that the wrong was done to one who loves him and who, instead of resenting the personal damage, has sorrowed for him that he should have been capable of it, and has no other desire than his redemption. That turns his heart. It shows him the blackness of his transgression, and reveals it to him as not merely a violation of law but an outrage upon Love. It delivers him from the grip of Conscience, but at the same time it imposes on him a weightier obligation, a debt of gratitude which an eternity of devotion could not discharge.

The Sacrifice of the Atonement.

And this is the Atonement. Christ was the Eternal Son of God, one with the Father in thought and purpose; and when He made Himself one with us and suffered for our sins, the Righteous for the unrighteous, it was a discovery of the anguish which our evil behaviour has cost our Father. And in presence of that Love which we have wounded and which has never ceased sorrowing over us and yearning after us, we bow in contrition and humbly confess our sin. And we accept its free forgiveness with no thought of reparation, of just amends and legal quittance, but with the sense of an immeasurable obligation. 'For the love of Christ constraineth us; because we thus judge, that One died for all, therefore all died; and He died for all, that they which live should no longer live unto themselves, but unto Him who for their sakes died and rose again.' This is the one way of peace; and it is the way which the Love of God in Christ Jesus our Lord has opened for every penitent sinner.

2 Cor. v. 14, 15.

(3) IMPUTATION AND HEREDITY

> ' Why should the private pleasure of some one
> Become the public plague of many moe ?
> Let sin, alone committed, light alone
> Upon his head that hath transgressed so ;
> Let guiltless souls be freed from guilty woe :
> For one's offence why should so many fall,
> To plague a private sin in general ? '
>
> SHAKESPEARE.

Atonement in
the light of
Divine
Fatherhood.

THE parable of the Prodigal Son is the *locus classicus* of our Lord's soteriological teaching ; and we have learned from it the large and momentous truth, that God is the Universal Father, and the Atonement must be construed in these terms. It has ruled out the old conceptions of God as the Moral Governor of the world requiring satisfaction for His violated honour, and the King and Judge of men exacting the penalty which legal justice demands ; and it has defined the Atonement as a Father's dealing with His erring children. And thus it has discovered the true significance of our Lord's Sacrifice for the sin of the world. This is not, according to the pagan notion, a

propitiation to appease the divine wrath. It
is Love's Sacrifice, the burden which His
children's sin lays upon the Heavenly Father's
heart. And the parable has shown us not
only the necessity of that Sacrifice but its
efficacy. It was necessary, since Love is in
its very nature a vicarious principle, and when
His children sinned it was inevitable that the
Father should sorrow for them and suffer
with them. And it is efficacious, inasmuch
as it satisfies the soul's moral instinct, its
demand for expiation. So long as sin is
construed in legal terms as a crime, there is
no peace for the sinner until he has endured
the penalty and, in the Scottish phrase,
' tholed assize ' ; but when it is recognised
as an outrage upon Love, then the obligation of reparation ceases and gives place
to the instinct of gratitude. The Love
which has suffered for our sin enkindles in
our breasts an answering love, an eternal
devotion.

This is the doctrine of the Atonement in
terms of the Christian master-truth of the
Fatherhood of God. And truly it is a noble
and moving doctrine. Yet it is incomplete ;

No provision
for human
infirmity.

and its defect is this, that it makes no provision for human infirmity. The discovery of the Love of God in Christ Jesus our Lord opens to us a way of access to our Father, and assures us of His free and overflowing welcome and His remission and oblivion of our evil past. But sin has corrupted and weakened our souls, and mere remission of the sin of the past is no safeguard against its recurrence in the future and no guarantee that our weak hearts will fulfil their purpose of grateful devotion. In theological phrase, Justification is insufficient ; it must be followed by Sanctification. Of course Sanctification is an office of the Holy Spirit, and it may be argued that it does not belong to our Lord's work of Atonement ; but it must be considered that the Holy Spirit's ministry is nothing else than an application of the work of Christ, and the latter is all-embracing and comprehends our salvation from first to last. The Father works through the Son, and the Holy Spirit's office is the unfolding of His grace and the enforcement of His Infinite Sacrifice. Thus it is God who forgives, but He forgives in Christ ; and it is the Holy Spirit who sanctifies, but

He sanctifies in Christ. Hence it is written that Christ ' was made unto us wisdom from God, and righteousness and sanctification, and redemption.' 1 Cor. i. 30.

The doctrine of the Fatherhood of God shows movingly how Christ was made unto us ' redemption,' but it does not show how He was made unto us ' righteousness and sanctification.' Our Lord indeed recognised the latter necessity, and He proclaimed it when He spoke of sin as a disease and salvation as healing. ' They that are whole have no need of a physician, but they that are sick.' If sin were merely a crime, it might suffice to cancel it and grant the sinner a fresh start ; but since it is rather a disease, it is not the past alone but the future also that must be considered. The sinner needs healing, and God must perform the office of a physician. It would suffice for a ruler to proclaim an amnesty and, in Turrettin's phrase, ' relax the law ' and forgo the execution of its penalty ; but a physician must heal the sufferer and rid him of the malady which has afflicted him in the past and, unless it be eradicated, will afflict him still. Our Lord's recognition of this necessity.

Mt. ix. 12.

The Pauline doctrine of Imputation.

Rom. v. 18, 19.

1 Cor. xv. 21, 22.

An ancient problem.

And how is this necessity met by the work of our Lord ?   The answer is furnished by the Pauline doctrine of Imputation : ' As through one trespass the judgment came unto all men to condemnation ; even so through one act of righteousness the free gift came unto all men to justification of life.   For as through the one man's disobedience the many were made sinners, even so through the obedience of the One shall the many be made righteous.' 'Since by man came death, by man came also the resurrection of the dead.   For as in Adam all die, so also in Christ shall all be made alive.' There is here a twofold imputation : on the one side the imputation of Adam's sin to his posterity, and on the other the imputation of Christ's righteousness to believers ; and for many a generation it presented an obstinate problem to theologians.

In the fifth century Pelagius stoutly denied the *damnosa hæreditas* of Adam's sin, maintaining that there is no *tradux peccati*, no entail of guilt, no hereditary curse.   He was encountered by St. Augustine, but the latter's arguments were far from decisive and indeed served only to open fresh controversies.

' Nothing,' confesses Calvin,[1] ' is more remote from common sense than that all should become guilty for the fault of one, and thus sin become common. And this seems to have been the reason with the most ancient teachers why they touched only obscurely on this head ; at all events, why they explained it less clearly than was adequate.' The problem so unsuccessfully handled by the Fathers was resumed by ' the men of the new learning,' but it still baffled even their acute intellects.

The Lutheran theologians sought a solution in a characteristically subtle definition of the term ' Imputation.' They recognised a twofold possibility. The imputation of Adam's sin (*imputatio peccati Adamitici*) might be either ' immediate ' (*immediata*) or ' mediate ' (*mediata*). In the former case Adam's descendants were present and co-operative in his sin ; and this was affirmed by some on the theory that in his will all their wills were placed (*locatæ erant omnes voluntates posterorum*). The embarrassments of the theory are, however, extreme. It would imply the pre-existence of souls, and it would make

Lutheran solution: 'immediate' and 'mediate imputation.'

[1] *Instit.* II. i. 5.

Adam not a person but a personalisation of the race. And so the idea of 'immediate imputation' was generally rejected, and recourse was had to that of 'mediate imputation.' Adam was accounted not merely the physical but the moral head of humanity, the representative of the race; and thus whatever he did, it was as though the race had done it. But there still remained the question of the connection between him and his descendants—how they could be charged with responsibility for his sin though they had no part in it either by commission or by consent; and an answer was proposed by David Hollaz in the latter half of the seventeenth century. He introduced the idea of ' God's middle knowledge ' (*scientia Dei media*) or ' knowledge of futurity ' (*scientia futuribilium*), signifying that, since God knew that in Adam's place his descendants would have acted precisely as he did, it was therefore just that they should be accounted partakers of his sin. Contingent guilt was treated as actual guilt.[1]

[1] *Cf.* Turrett. *Instit. Theol.* IX. ix; Dorner, *Syst.* ii. pp. 350 ff.

The Calvinistic theologians also addressed themselves to the problem of Imputation ; and the solution which they proposed was the system known as the Federal Theology. Though its idea had been previously enunciated, especially by Calvin's contemporary, Heinrich Bullinger of Zürich, in his work *De Testamento seu Fœdere Dei Unico et Eterno* (1534), the distinction of founding the system belongs to that master of theology and exegesis, Robert Rollock, Principal of the University of Edinburgh (1555-1599). It was adopted by the early English Puritans, and it is presented in the Westminster Confession of Faith (1643) ; [1] but it was somewhat later that it received its classic exposition from two Dutch theologians—Johannes Cocceius (Koch), a pupil of William Ames (Amesius) and Professor of Theology at Leyden (b. 1603, d. 1669), in his work *Summa Doctrinæ de Fœdere et Testamento Dei* (1648), and his follower, Hermann Witsius, Professor at Utrecht, in his work *De Œconomia Fœderum Dei cum Hominibus* (1671).

The Calvinistic solution : the Federal Theology.

[1] Chap. vii.—Of God's Covenant with Man. *Cf*. Larger Catech., Q. 22.

The Covenant of Works and the Covenant of Grace.

It was an attempt, and a highly meritorious attempt, to interpret the history of Redemption in terms of the Pauline doctrine of Imputation. It introduced the idea of a federal relationship between Adam and his posterity in virtue of ' a covenant of works ' which, it was conceived, he had contracted with God in his own name and also in theirs. In this covenant, say the Westminster Divines, ' life was promised to Adam, and in him to his posterity, upon condition of perfect and personal obedience '; and when he violated it, his descendants to the remotest generation were involved in the fatal consequences of his disobedience. ' The covenant being made with Adam as a publick person, not for himself only, but for his posterity, all mankind descending from him by ordinary generation sinned in him, and fell with him in that first transgression.' Such is the *rationale* of the Imputation of Adam's sin ; and the disaster was retrieved in like manner by a second covenant and a second imputation—the Covenant of Grace, and the Imputation of Christ's Righteousness. ' Man by his fall having made himself incapable of life by that covenant, the Lord was pleased to make a second, commonly called the Covenant of Grace : whereby he freely offereth unto sinners life and salvation by Jesus Christ, requiring of them faith in him, that they may be saved ; and promising to give unto all those that are ordained unto life his Holy Spirit to make them willing and able to believe.'

The Federal Theology is indeed a noble conception, and it claims abiding reverence for the service which it rendered in its day to evangelical religion ; nevertheless it is no adequate solution of the problem. Its basal idea is liable to two fatal objections. One is that it lacks scriptural sanction. For the Scriptures nowhere mention a primal covenant between God and Adam, but merely a command and a warning ; and these concerned Adam alone.[1] And not only is the primal covenant a dogmatic fiction, but the idea of a covenant with Adam binding his posterity as well as himself is an impracticable notion.

Two objections.

Cf. Gen. ii. 16, 17.

[1] According to the Scriptures the first Covenant was the covenant with Israel at Sinai (Ex. xxiv. 4-8)—'the covenant that I made with their fathers in the day that I took them by the hand to bring them out of the land of Egypt' (Jer. xxxi. 32).

A representative may pledge his constituents, but it is their commission that constitutes him their representative ; and Adam held no commission from generations yet unborn. It would be the extremity of injustice that the race should be laid under obligation by a covenant which it had never approved.

The scientific solution : Heredity and Solidarity.

Here the problem was left by the theologians, and it remained a mystery until in recent days Physical Science, prosecuting her investigation of the Book of Nature, ' that universal and public manuscript that lies expans'd unto the eyes of all,' discovered there the Law of Heredity and the companion principle of the Solidarity of the Human Race.

> ' Born into life !—man grows
>   Forth from his parents' stem,
>   And blends their bloods, as those
>   Of theirs are blent in them ;
> So each new man strikes root into a far fore-time.
>
> ' Born into life !—we bring
>   A bias with us here,
>   And, when here, each new thing
>   Affects us we come near ;
> To tunes we did not call our being must keep chime.'

Thus the generations are inter-related, and each is the heir of its predecessor. This is the Law of Heredity. And according to the principle of Solidarity humanity is an organism, and no member is isolated but each shares the common life. And so generations and individuals are linked together.

The operation of the principle is twofold. On the one hand, it involves a heavy curse. ' The iniquity of the fathers is visited upon the children '; and even where there is no community of blood, the innocent suffer for the guilty, and the inevitable penalty falls oftentimes most heavily where it is undeserved. ' So deeply inherent is it in this life of ours that men have to suffer for each other's sins, so inevitably diffusive is human suffering, that even justice makes its victims, and we can conceive no retribution that does not spread beyond its mark in pulsations of unmerited pain.' [1] Here is the justification of the Apostle's doctrine of the imputation of Adam's sin. Adam was the father of the race, and his sin is the heritage of his children from generation to generation. The stream of life was poisoned at its source, and it has gathered in its course ever fresh pollution.

The entail of evil.

[1] George Eliot, *The Mill on the Floss*, III. vii.

N

The entail of goodness.

But the principle has another aspect, as beneficent as that is stern and cruel. There is an entail of goodness no less than an entail of evil. If the child inherits the curse of his parents' sin, he inherits also the benediction of their righteousness ; and each heroic sacrifice, each noble achievement, is a possession of the race. No effort, no aspiration is ever futile ; and the world is the better and the purer at this hour not alone for its heroes and martyrs but for the multitude of nameless and forgotten folk who have lived and loved and laboured in it, unnoticed and unapplauded. ' For the growing good of the world is partly dependent on unhistoric acts ; and that things are not so ill with you and me as they might have been, is half owing to the number who lived faithfully a hidden life, and rest in unvisited tombs.' [1]

The doctrine of Imputation.

And this principle finds its supreme expression in the imputation of Christ's righteousness. He was the Second Adam, the new Head of humanity ; and even as the First Adam's sin has defiled the life-stream of succeeding generations, so there is healing

[1] George Eliot, *Middlemarch*, ad finem.

for the race in the Second Adam's righteousness. And thus we are heirs of a double entail. There are two fountains and two streams, one poisoned and the other medicinal ; and the hope of humanity, the promise of its final and full redemption, lies in this—that the stream of healing is mightier than the stream of death. Mercy is stronger than judgment and reaches farther. The entail of righteousness endures long after the entail of sin is spent, as it was written of old : ' I the Lord thy God am a jealous God, visiting the iniquity of the fathers upon the children, *upon the third and upon the fourth generation* of them that hate Me ; and showing mercy *unto a thousand generations* of them that love Me and keep My commandments.'

Ex. xx. 5, 6, R.V. marg.

(4) MAN'S OFFERING TO GOD

' My faith would lay her hand
   On that dear head of Thine,
While like a penitent I stand,
   And there confess my sin.

' Believing, we rejoice
   To see the curse remove ;
We bless the Lamb with cheerful voice,
   And sing His bleeding love.'

ISAAC WATTS.

Active and Passive Obedience. THERE is an old *quæstio theologicalis* which emerges here with a new import. It distinguished between our Lord's Active and His Passive Obedience. The former signifies all that He *did* in fulfilment of the Law throughout the course of His earthly life ; and the latter all that He *suffered*, His voluntary Passion for the sin of the world. And the question which was keenly and indeed acrimoniously debated by the Post-Reformation theologians, was what constituted, as the phrase was, the *materia satisfactionis* ; whether His Atoning Sacrifice was limited to

His Passive Obedience or comprised His
Active Obedience too.[1]

The former opinion was maintained by
a party owning as its chief representative
the Reformed theologian Johannes Piscator
(Fischer), Professor of Theology at Herborn
(b. 1546, d. 1625). Its advocates, however,
were not completely unanimous. They
agreed that it was His Passive Obedience that
constituted Christ's Atoning Sacrifice, but
'some of them,' says Turrettin, 'put righteousness entirely in the Death of Christ, while
others join thereto all the sufferings which
He endured during His entire lifetime, and
this they call " passive righteousness " ; and
as for His " active righteousness," which they
place in the obedience which He rendered
to the commandments, they account that it
was as a requisite condition in the person
of the Mediator for the execution of His
office, but forms no part of the satisfaction
or the merit which is imputed to us. But,'
continues Turrettin, ' the common and received opinion in our Churches is that the

Both comprised in our Lord's Atoning Sacrifice.

[1] *Cf.* Turrettin, *Instit. Theol.* XIV. xiii : *De Materia
Satisfactionis.*

Satisfaction of Christ which is imputed to us for righteousness before God, embraces not only Christ's sufferings which He endured whether in death or in life, but also the obedience of His whole life, or the righteous and holy actions by which He perfectly fulfilled the commandments of the Law in our place ; so that from these two parts the entire and perfect price of our redemption arises.'

Scriptural emphasis on His Death.

This old controversy involves a principle of vital consequence ; and it is well that the Reformed theologians decided as they did, and recognised in the Atoning Sacrifice not merely our Lord's Passive but His Active Obedience, not merely His death on the Cross nor yet merely, in addition thereto, all the sufferings of His mortal condition, but His whole life of devotion to the Father's will. Is this, however, the doctrine of the New Testament ? There are two words of our Lord which, from the circumstances amid which they were spoken, claim peculiarly reverent consideration. One is His word to the Twelve when He was going up to Jerusalem to die : ' The Son of Man came not to be ministered unto, but to minister, and to

Mt. xx. 28.

give His life a ransom for many.' And the
other is His declaration at the institution of
the Holy Supper in the Upper Room the same
night in which He was betrayed : ' This is   xxvi. 28.
My blood of the Covenant, which is shed for
many unto remission of sins.'   Here it is
especially with His Death—the giving of His
life and the shedding of His blood—that He
connects redemption and remission.   And
with this the apostolic teaching accords.
' If,' says St. Paul, ' while we were enemies,   Rom. v. 10.
we were reconciled to God through the death
of His Son, much more, being reconciled,
shall we be saved by His life.'   Again : ' We   Eph. i. 7.
have our redemption through His blood, the
forgiveness of our trespasses.'   And again :
' It was the good pleasure of the Father . . .   Col. i. 19, 20.
through Him to reconcile all things unto Him-
self, having made peace through the blood of
His Cross.'   And so it is written also in the
Epistle to the Hebrews : ' Having boldness   x. 19, 22.
to enter into the Holy Place by the blood of
Jesus . . . let us draw near.'   ' The blood of   1 Jo. i. 7.
Jesus His Son,' says St. John, ' cleanseth us
from all sin.'   ' Ye were redeemed,' says   1 Pet. i. 18, 19.
St. Peter, ' not with corruptible things . . .

but with precious blood, as of a lamb without blemish and without spot, even the blood of Christ.'

The reason: Here it is on our Lord's death that the emphasis is laid, and it seems as though the affirmation were that the atoning efficacy lies in His Passive Obedience. But this were a hasty inference ; and there are other passages which illuminate the apostolic thought, especially that word of St. Paul :

Phil. ii. 8, R.V. 'He humbled Himself, becoming obedient even unto death, yea, the death of the Cross.'

(1) His obedience His Sacrifice. Two essential truths are here implied. One is that it was His obedience to the Father's will that constituted our Lord's Atoning Sacrifice, in accordance with that lofty

x. 1-10. passage in the Epistle to the Hebrews, where it is contrasted with the ancient sacrifices and the reason of its superior efficacy indicated. 'It is impossible that the blood of bulls and goats should take away sins ' ; and our Lord's Sacrifice avails, not because His blood was nobler than theirs, but by reason of what the shedding of His blood signified—the absolute surrender of His will to God : 'by which will we have been sanctified through the offering

of the body of Jesus Christ once for all.'
There lies its efficacy—not in His death
simply but in His resolute obedience to the
Father's will, the steadfast devotion which
brought Him to that uttermost extremity.
And further, St. Paul affirms, that obedience (2) His obedience lifelong.
was lifelong. He 'became obedient even
unto death, yea, the death of the Cross.' At
every step of His progress through the world
He submitted to the Father's will, resolutely
treading the painful pathway to the Cross
and refusing to turn aside. His life was one His death its consummation.
long self-abnegation, and His death was its
consummation. His acquiescence in Gethse-
mane in presence of the last dread ordeal—
'O My Father, if it be possible, let this cup Mt. xxvi. 39.
pass away from Me : nevertheless, not as I
will, but as Thou wilt'—was His final act
of obedience, the climax of that self-devotion
which He had practised throughout His
earthly career.

Hence appears the reason why the New His whole life sacrificial.
Testament lays peculiar emphasis on His
Death. It was the crown of His Life; and His
Life was His Sacrifice—that Life of unbroken
obedience which was consummated by His

Death. And thus the poet has written, proclaiming the truth which theologians have too often missed :—

> ' Very dear the Cross of shame,
>   Where He took the sinner's blame,
>   And the tomb wherein the Saviour lay,
>   Until the third day came ;
>   Yet He bore the self-same load;
>   And He went the same high road,
>   When the carpenter of Nazareth
>   Made common things for God.'

1 Pet. ii. 24.

He ' bare our sins in His body,' as St. Peter has it according to the true rendering of his words,[1] ' right up to the Tree.' He bare them all the way from Bethlehem to Calvary, no less when He was handling hammer and saw in the carpenter's shop at Nazareth and telling the Glad Tidings or working gracious miracles in Galilee and Jerusalem than when He was hanging on the Cross. For all the

---

[1] τὰς ἁμαρτίας ἡμῶν αὐτὸς ἀνήνεγκεν (Is. liii. 12) ἐν τῷ σώματι αὐτοῦ ἐπὶ τὸ ξύλον, 'carried up our sins in His body to the Tree' (R.V. marg.). All the days of His flesh He was treading the *Via Dolorosa*, climbing the Hill of Calvary with His Cross on His back. ἐπὶ τὸ ξύλον can mean only 'on to the Tree' (*cf.* Acts x. 9). 'On the Tree' would be ἐπὶ τοῦ ξύλου (*cf.* Lk. iv. 29) or ἐπὶ τῷ ξύλῳ (*cf.* Mt. xiv. 11 ; Jo. iv. 6).

while He was obedient to the Father's will, and His obedience to the Father's will was His Sacrifice for the sin of the world.

And this ' obedience even unto death, yea, the death of the Cross,' is the righteousness of Christ which is imputed to sinners. It has already appeared how science has vindicated the doctrine of Imputation ; and now the question arises whether it does not follow, in accordance with the scientific interpretation, that imputation is an involuntary process, involving neither personal faith nor personal responsibility. It will at once define the problem and facilitate its solution if we revert to the ancient controversy. Pelagius, it will be remembered, rejected the idea of the imputation of Adam's sin to his posterity ; and his chief prejudice against it was inspired by one grim consequence which it seemed to involve—the reprobation of children who, born under the hereditary curse, died in infancy ere they were capable of saving faith. The hearts of the gracious heresiarch and his followers rebelled against this appalling dogma, which, they alleged, would render celibacy a duty, since it would be a crime to bring

Imputation and responsibility.

Unbaptized infants and Original Sin.

Pelagius.

children into being and expose them to the risk of such a doom.

St. Augustine.   St. Augustine dealt with the problem in the course of his Pelagian controversies, and it is instructive to observe how he hesitated and laboured to evade the dire inference. His notion of the hereditary curse precluded the admission of the salvation of unbaptized infants. They would bear the punishment of Adam's sin ; but, he argued, the punishment would be mitigated in their case. Their *damnatio* was inevitable, but it would be *damnatio levissima.* ' Who can doubt,' he cries,[1] ' that unbaptized children, who have only original sin and are not burdened with any of their own, will be in the lightest condemnation of all ? And though I cannot define of what sort and how great that will be, still I dare not say that it would be better for them that they did not exist than that they should be there.' From this illogical yet gracious reluctance to draw the full and inevitable inference arose the mediæval notion of the *Limbus Infantium*, which still maintains its place in Roman Catholic theology.

[1] *Contra Jul. Pel.* v. 44.

' We hold that, after the promulgation of the Gospel, infants who die without Baptism of water or of blood, are not admitted to the supernatural vision of God which constitutes the happiness of Heaven ; that in consequence of the sin of Adam, they will remain for ever deprived of that happiness for which they were destined. But this privation is no injustice to them, for their nature gave them no claim in justice to a supernatural reward ; nor does it imply any unhappiness in them, for they need not be supposed to know what they have lost.' [1]

The solution of the problem appears when the distinction between *sinfulness* and *guilt* is recognised. Sinfulness is hereditary. Every son of Adam is born with a nature corrupt and prone to evil ; but there is no guilt where there is no consent, and where there is no guilt there is no punishment. Sinfulness is hereditary, but guilt is not. The latter arises only when the will yields to the solicitation of evil and embraces it. And thus no unconscious infant is condemned for

Sinfulness and guilt.

[1] Sylvester J. Hunter, S.J., *Outlines of Catholic Theology*, 696.

Adam's sin, and the divine judgment in every case will be not absolute but relative. It will have regard not simply to the issue but to the conflict ; and its severity will be Lk. xii. 47, 48. measured by opportunity. 'That servant, which knew his lord's will, and made not ready, nor did according to his will, shall be beaten with many stripes ; but he that knew not, and did things worthy of stripes, shall be beaten with few stripes.' It is the will that counts ; and in God's sight there is more merit in a struggle, albeit unsuccessful, against hereditary propensities to evil than in the facile virtue of one whose blood is clean and whose environment is propitious.

Imputation and faith.

This is the principle of the imputation of Adam's sin ; and it is equally the principle of the imputation of Christ's righteousness. His righteousness becomes ours, in the Pauline phrase, 'by faith' ; and faith signifies the will's consent and the affection's embracement. It is indeed true that the imputation alike of sin and of righteousness is an involuntary process. The sin of Adam has infected the race, and rendered the moral conflict harder for us all ; and, conversely, the righteousness of Christ is perpetually leavening the corporate life of humanity and purifying and ennobling it from generation to generation.   And thus it is written that He is ' an atonement for our sins ; and not for ours only, but also for the whole world.'   But even as it is the consent of our wills to Adam's sin that condemns us, so it is the consent of our wills to Christ's righteousness that justifies us.   And thus it is written again that God is ' the Saviour of all men, specially of them that believe.'

Here is the personal factor in Imputation. The Atonement is God's Sacrifice for the sin of the world, but it is also man's offering to God ; and until we make it our offering we remain strangers to its personal efficacy.   Christ has realised by His perfect obedience to the Father's will the ideal life of humanity ; and the moment our wills consent to all that He was and did, and our souls bow before Him in reverence and penitence and desire, confessing our own failures and yielding ourselves to the grace of His Holy Spirit, that moment we are one with Him, and His righteousness is imputed to us.

1 Jo. ii. 2.

1 Tim. iv. 10.

God's Sacrifice and man's offering.

THE WORD OF RECONCILIATION

O

THE WORD OF RECONCILIATION

> ' I love to tell the story :
>   More wonderful it seems
> Than all the golden fancies
>   Of all my golden dreams.
> I love to tell the story :
>   It did so much for me :
> And that is just the reason
>   I tell it now to thee.'
>
> KATHERINE HANKEY.

THE practical test of a doctrine of the Atone-ment is its suitability for preaching, its efficacy as a message of salvation, its power of commending to sinners, in Bunyan's poignant phrase, ' the want and worth of Jesus Christ to save them ' and ' enabling them to venture their souls upon Him.'   And now that we have reached the end of our argument, let us review the road which we have travelled and take account of the treasures which we have gathered by the way and the evangelical gains which they afford.

The first is a tender and gracious thought of God, an illumination of that truth which

Evangelical gains:

1. An alluring thought of God.

is the distinctive message of the Epistle to the Hebrews, that the supreme blessing of the Gospel is freedom of access to God, Heb. x. 19, 20, 22. 'boldness to enter into the Holy Place by the blood of Jesus, by the way which He dedicated for us, a new and living way, through the veil, that is to say, His flesh,' so that we may 'draw near with a true heart in fulness of faith.' Perfect love has cast out fear. The difference is well illustrated by an incident which a godly mother once related from her own experience. She was talking with her little daughter of salvation, and she explained that it meant 'loving God.' 'But,' answered the child, 'I don't love God. I love Jesus, but I am afraid of God.' There lay the mischief of the old doctrine. Despite every attempt to evade it the fact remained that a wide gulf was fixed between God and Christ. God was the stern and awful Judge, and Christ the merciful Saviour who interposed and received on His own meek head the inexorable stroke of the divine wrath.

This thought of God is a grim nightmare, and it vanishes in the light of the Christian revelation. Think of Jesus as He is portrayed on the pages of the New Testament,

> ' How He walked here, the shadow of Him Love,
> The speech of Him soft Music, and His step
> A Benediction.'

Think of that face which ' ministered life to the beholders,' the kindest the world has ever seen ; that gracious voice, the sweetest the world has ever heard ; that hand which was never lifted save in blessing ; that heart which overflowed with pity and broke for desire of us on the Cross. At the very thought of Him our poor souls leap up in faith and longing, and we wish that He were in our midst still that we might go to Him, and tell Him our need and sorrow and sin, and lay our burdens at His blessed feet. Only to be near Him were rest and peace, and we would never be afraid of anything that He might do to us. And here is the wonderful truth : Jesus was ' the Visible Image of the Invisible God,' and when we see Him, we see God. The heart of the Eternal Father was manifested in the Incarnate Son ; and the Love which dwelt here long ago is the Power which holds us evermore in its benignant grasp, thinking of us, planning for us, ordering our lives, and appointing our destinies. When we see Jesus, we see God. His Love was the Father's Love, and His Sacrifice the Father's Sacrifice. Christ Crucified is God bearing the sin of the world.

2. An encouragement to faith :

And hence emerges a compelling argument for faith, emboldening sinners to appropriate salvation and rest upon it with assured confidence. The old question whether Christ died for all or only for the elect, is for ever ruled out. For the Atonement is the Father's Sacrifice, and His Fatherhood is as wide as humanity. All the children of men are His children, and the Cross is the revelation of His sorrow for their sin and His yearning for their recovery.

For the awakened sinner.

This truth is the very heart of the Gospel ; and if it were more clearly perceived and more firmly grasped, there would be less misgiving in awakened souls, less lack of ' assurance,' and a braver and more joyful faith. It is indeed a truth which it is needful to bear in mind from beginning to end of the Christian life. It opens the way for a penitent at his first approach to the Saviour, and shows him his title to enter into peace. It tells him that there is no question whether God will forgive him, since his forgiveness is already a *fait accompli* ; and the only question is whether he will appropriate the mercy which is assured him and enter in at the door which stands open for him and every sinner of mankind. Christ was God manifest in the flesh, and He died for the world and attested for ever the thoughts and purposes of the Eternal Father's heart. And hence, as the saintly McLeod Campbell expressed it, the Gospel message is not ' Believe that Christ died for you, and your faith will be an evidence to yourself that you are one of those for whom He died,' but rather ' Believe that Christ died for you, because He died for all mankind ' ; it is not ' Believe in the forgiveness of your sins, *and they will be* forgiven,' but rather ' Believe in the forgiveness of your sins *because they are* forgiven.' The Atonement is not merely a declaration of God's willingness to forgive ; it is an abiding evidence that the sin of the world has been expiated by God's Infinite Sacrifice, and forgiveness to the uttermost is assured to every sinner who will receive it. Forgiveness is ours already *de jure*, and it becomes ours *de facto* the moment we claim it. The invitation, the command of the Gospel is not ' Believe, and your sin will be forgiven,' but ' Your sin is forgiven, therefore believe ; appropriate your blood-bought heritage.' It is indeed possible that we may miss forgiveness ; but if we do, let us understand the reason. It is not that there was no forgiveness for us, but that forgiveness full and free was ours, and we would not accept it. Was not that our Lord's word ? ' O Jerusalem, Jerusalem ! how often would I have gathered thy children together, even as a hen gathereth her chickens under her wings, *and ye would not* !'

Mt. xxiii. 37.

For the backsliding believe.

This is the golden secret of peace, the sovereign encouragement of the awakened sinner, emboldening him to trust and be at peace. And it is no less precious to the backslider. After we have believed and accepted forgiveness we too often relapse into sin ; and then we fancy that our past acceptance counts for nothing, and all must begin anew. But this is a limitation of God's Infinite

Sacrifice in Christ. He bore in His vicarious love the burden of the whole world's sin, not the sins of the past only but every sin of every sinner to the uttermost of time. He knew the end from the beginning, and all the long tale of human transgression lay in His view and He felt the anguish of it all. No new sin which invades our lives, ever takes Him by surprise. It was foreseen by Him ; and when first we bowed in penitence before the Cross, He accepted us for ever and ever ; He forgave the sin of yesterday, and the sin of the morrow, and the sin of each succeeding day to the close of our earthly pilgrimage. And thus the Christian life is a continual returning to the Mercy-seat and reappropriation of the inexhaustible grace which healed us at the first and still avails for each fresh wound.

And, finally, the doctrine of the Atonement, as we have sought feebly to define it in the light of the larger thought which is the Holy Spirit's gift to our generation, lays a strong restraint on sin and provides an inspiring incentive to holiness. It enforces that saying of the Apostle that 'none of us liveth to

3. A restraint of sin and an incentive to holiness.

Rom. xiv. 7.

The transmission of evil.

himself.'[1]   By the law of Imputation the sin of each passes beyond the narrow limits of his own life and poisons every life that is in contact with his, travelling outward in an ever-widening circle.   It is an augmentation of the stream of corruption which originated in the primal transgression and has flowed in growing volume down the course of the ages. And once this solemn truth is perceived, it is impossible to sin with a light heart.   It rings in our ears like the despairing cry of 'that miserable mortal,' Francis Spiera, which was as knives and daggers in Bunyan's soul : ' Man knows the beginning of sin, but who bounds the issues thereof ? '

The transmission of goodness.

The transmission of sin, however, is only one side of the law of Imputation, and the other side is the transmission of righteousness. Good no less than evil is pervasive ; and each true act, each noble word, each holy aspiration is a widening of the borders of light. Nay, just as our evil is a reinforcement of the first Adam's sin, so our goodness is a reinforcement of the Second Adam's righteousness.

[1] *Cf.* Sen. *De Vit. Beat.* i : 'Nemo sibi tantummodo errat sed alieni erroris et causa et auctor est.'

St. Paul has affirmed this truth in language which might seem impious on other lips than an inspired Apostle's. 'I rejoice,' he wrote Col. i. 24. to the Colossians, 'in my sufferings for your sake, and fill up on my part that which is lacking of the afflictions of Christ in my flesh for His Body's sake, which is the Church.' The Father's Sacrifice is agelong. The Cross was a revelation in time of the anguish which the sin of the world costs Him evermore. From the hour of sin's entrance He has been bearing His children's griefs and carrying their sorrows ; and ere ever the Cross was set up on Calvary there was an unseen Cross in Heaven. And hence the prophet wrote of old that 'in all their affliction He was Is. lxiii. 9. afflicted,' and the seer in Patmos spoke of 'the Lamb that hath been slain from the Rev. xiii. 8. foundation of the world.' The Vicarious Sacrifice began when sin appeared, nor will it ever cease until sin has been purged from the world. The Heart which was broken on Calvary is breaking still, and the Redeemer's Passion is continued from age to age in the Church which is His Body, His perpetual Incarnation. And thus His challenge abides

Mt. xvi. 24.

from generation to generation : ' If any man would come after Me, let him deny himself, and take up his cross, and follow Me.' And when we loyally respond, and take up our daily burdens, and bear them in the dear Lord's faith and love, then we are His comrades on the Sorrowful Road, partners, after our little measure, in His Atoning Sacrifice, His fellow-labourers for the redemption of the world.

INDEXES

I

SUBJECTS AND NAMES

II

PASSAGES OF SCRIPTURE

Printed in Great Britain by T. and A. Constable, Printers to His Majesty
at the Edinburgh University Press

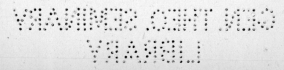